What r⸻

TV portrays the typica⸻ ⸻usband as an inept and ignorant klutz, while the stereotype bachelor is a macho Rambo and a lady-killer.

But what is a man, *really?*

In **Real Men Do**, Dr. Ken Olson shares his pilgrimage into understanding what being a man is all about. Through personal self-examination and professional insight as a psychologist, Dr. Olson reveals the makeup of a man in down-to-earth terms. He discloses important truths that both men and women ought to know concerning manhood:

- *expressing (and suppressing) emotions*
- *what boys are subconsciously programmed to know about women*
- *a man's vulnerable areas*
- *friendship and loneliness*
- *depression, stress, and illness*
- *work priorities*
- *intimacy and sexual fulfillment in marriage*
- *a man's role as a father*
- *the hazards of middle age*
- *resolving marital conflicts*
- *retirement plans*

REAL
MEN
DO

By Dr. Ken Olson

Real Men Do

The Art of Hanging Loose in an Uptight World

Can You Wait Till Friday? The Psychology of Hope

I Hurt Too Much for a Band-Aid

REAL MEN DO

ken olson

Fleming H. Revell Company
Old Tappan, New Jersey

Library of Congress Cataloging in Publication Data

Olson, Ken.
  Real men do.

  Bibliography: p.
  1. Men—Religious life. 2. Men (Christian theology)
—Popular works. I. Title.
BV4843.O47 1987   248.8'42   87-9731
ISBN 0-8007-5243-0

Copyright © 1978, 1987 by Kenneth J. Olson
Published by the Fleming H. Revell Company
Old Tappan, New Jersey 07675
Printed in the United States of America

I would like to dedicate this book
to every man who will read it
and then say, "Why not!
I begin my own pilgrimage now."

CONTENTS

Part I: Introduction

1   The Beginning of a Pilgrimage   13

Part II: The Making of a Man

2   How You Are Programmed   27
3   The Development of Masculinity   35
4   It's So Hard to Cry   52
5   A Man's Mistress: His Work!   67

Part III: Vulnerability

6   The Vulnerability of Success and Failure   81
7   The Crisis of the Middle-Aged Man   94
8   When a Man Is Sick   107
9   Do I Have to Die When I Retire?   119

Part IV: Relationships

10   It's Not Good for Man to Be Alone   127
11   Why Is It So Hard to Talk?   137
12   Passion and the Decision to Love   148
13   Intimacy in Marriage   158
14   The Healing of Relationships   169

Contents

15 Sex and Frustrated Lovers 185
16 They Call Me Dad 206

Part V: Conclusion

17 Spiritually Alive 225
   Source Notes 245

REAL
MEN
DO

INTRODUCTION

part one

—1—
THE BEGINNING OF A PILGRIMAGE

He who is not busy being born is busy dying.—Bob Dylan

I am a man on a pilgrimage to discover the most important truths about myself. At times in this very personal story I risk being open to you in the hope that my sharing will help you risk being more open, especially if you are a man. When I share my personal story, it is not because I am a famous or important person but only a pilgrim who believes that each bird whistles through his own beak. Since I sing my own song, you don't have to agree with anything I say. Just find your song and sing it.

To be honest, I have to admit that my pilgrimage has been at best characterized by erratic starts and stops. When I was not engaged in introspective soul searching to "know myself," I have been busy rushing through life and periodically suffering "burn out" from addiction to work.

One of my goals in life is growth, not perfection. This provides me with an inner motivation that will never be satisfied. As long as I am growing, I know that I am alive. I know I'm not perfect so there could never be a goal of perfection for me. I have learned how to trust what I think and feel inside and give myself permission to say, "Why not?" and risk making a mistake and failing. When I make mistakes, I don't call *myself* a mistake. I can fail but I'm not a failure.

Living One Day at a Time

One of the things I am still trying to learn is to live one day at a time. There are no trains to yesterday. I can't go back and change the past; it's gone. I can set goals for the future, build dreams for the future, and have hope for the future, but the only day I can live is today.

I once spoke at the State Dental Hygiene Convention in New Orleans, Louisiana. My hostess for the day invited me to join her family for a real Cajun meal. This family even had their own crawfish pond. There were nine girls in the family and when I met the youngest girl, I asked her how she felt about being the youngest and how old she was. She told me that she was seven and that she didn't like being the youngest. She said, "I hate being seven."

I said, "I know it must seem like it will never be your turn, and with eight older sisters ahead of you, you wonder if there will be anything left for you when it's your turn."

She said, "That's right."

"Well, I want to tell you a great secret of life, and if you can learn this secret, it will help you be very wise; maybe you'll be the wisest person in the family."

Her eyes sparkled and she asked, "What's the secret?"

As an answer I created this little poem for her:

PILGRIMAGE

When you are seven
It's like being in heaven
And when you are eight
It will be just great.
When you are nine
It will be just fine,
Because you've learned to live
One day at a time.

She listened so intently and then gave me a great big hug. After dinner she crawled up on my lap and repeated the poem, and so she learned this secret of life that made her very wise.

Fear of Rejection

As my pilgrimage into myself progressed, I wondered: if I was so sure I wanted to reveal myself openly and honestly, why was I having a difficult time writing this book? I discovered that I have a difficult time looking at me when there are things about me I don't want to see. I found so often that what I had discovered were only illusions about myself to protect and reassure myself that all was well with me. When I discovered some things about myself that I didn't like, I balked at putting my faults and weaknesses on paper for everyone to know.

Ever since I was a child, I realized, I have been on a pilgrimage to solve a deep mystery about myself. I don't remember how old I was when I discovered in me a certain funny feeling that I was not OK. I wondered what I had done to make me feel so ashamed and guilty. When I looked for the bad thing I had done to make me feel so unworthy inside, it slowly dawned on me that I had never done anything bad enough to make me feel this way, so maybe I was a "bad seed."

I remembered how painfully shy I was as a little boy. I hung my head down, ashamed, and I never looked anyone in the eye. My fear was that if someone looked me in the eye, they could see inside me and would discover my secret, that I was a bad seed.

Before my mother died of cancer, she had all five of her grown children come to the house. She had a large, beautiful collection of Royal Danish figurines. She had decided which ones she wanted to give to each of us. Mom said, "I want to make sure that Kenny gets the figurine of a young boy about three years old with his head hanging down. She said, "That's Kenny." It even looked like me, with thick blond hair. In his right hand he was dragging a teddy bear. Ironically, when I was a little boy, my parents would ask what I wanted for Christmas and I always asked for a teddy bear. Now I finally got my teddy bear.

A Drive for Approval

The fear of rejection and the certain funny feeling that I was not OK created in me a drive for the approval of others, especially my father, to reassure me that I was OK as a person. I was a compliant child who never rocked the boat or made waves by showing anger or by being disobedient.

Psychology books often say how important it is for your mental health, to accept and love yourself. It sounds so right and easy to say but in reality it is so hard to accomplish. Carl Jung wrote these powerful words in *Modern Man in Search of a Soul*.

Perhaps this sounds very simple, but simple things are always the most difficult. In actual life it requires the greatest discipline to be simple, and the acceptance of oneself is the essence of the moral problem and the epitome of a whole outlook upon life. That I feed the hungry, that I forgive an insult, that I love my enemy in the name of Christ—all these are undoubtedly great virtues. What I do unto the least of my brethren, that I do unto Christ. But what if I should discover that the least among them all, the poorest of all, the offenders, the very enemy himself, that these are within me, and that I myself am the enemy who must be loved—what then? As a rule, the Christian's attitude is then reversed; there is no longer any question of love or long-suffering; we say to the brother within us, "Raca (foul) and condemn and rage against ourselves. We hide it from the world; we refuse to admit even having met the least among the lowly in ourselves."[1]

What a powerful realization that "I myself am the enemy who must be loved." In years of counseling with wounded people, I have found that they have a very difficult time in forgiving themselves. Instead of forgiveness, there is a destructive name calling and cursing of oneself. A person will call himself dirty names that he would never allow his worst enemy to call him and get away with it.

It is strange how some of us will embrace guilt and never release it to God. In fact, some people become "blame blotters" and readily accept the blame and guilt that doesn't belong to them. Too often when we are suffering from guilt, we become our own judge and jury and even self-inflict the pain of punishment. Self-forgiveness is not even considered as an option. Forgiveness by God is refused because we feel if God really knew us, He wouldn't forgive us. No one knows us like God the Father, and His love and tender mercy to us while we are really messed up is overwhelming.

The most powerful story of the mercy and the forgiving heart of God is the story of the prodigal son's father. When the prodigal son finally came to his senses about himself, he decided to go home and say, " 'Father, I have sinned against both heaven and you and am no longer worthy of being called your son. Please take me on as a hired man.'

"So he returned home to his father. And while he was still

a long distance away, his father saw him coming, and was filled with loving pity and ran and embraced him and kissed him.

"His son said to him, 'Father, I have sinned against heaven and you and am not worthy of being called your son—'But his father said to the slaves, 'Quick! Bring the finest robe in the house and put it on him, and a jeweled ring for his finger; and shoes! And kill the calf we have in the fattening pen. We must celebrate with a feast, for this son of mine was dead and has returned to life. He was lost and is found.' So the party began" (Luke 15:18–24).

Wow! When one of us who has been lost and living a life of sin returns to God and asks His forgiveness, God throws a party in heaven for the one who is lost and who has come back home to Him.

The Need for Self-Acceptance

One day an honor-roll student in his junior year in high school was admitted to a psychiatric hospital in which I was conducting group therapy for young adults. Jerry was experiencing the terrifying living nightmare of a very bad psychiatric trip on LSD. He "knew" he was dead, and the sound of a tractor working outside convinced him that his grave was being dug.

Over the days, I tried to encourage Jerry to try living even if it meant only going swimming in the pool. He steadfastly refused because he believed there were poisonous rays coming out of his body that would poison the water and kill anyone else in the pool. As he was heavily medicated with Thorazine, he was like a zombie in group therapy.

About a week after admission to the hospital, Jerry began to regress and soon he lost his ability to walk. Another week went by, and he lost his ability to talk. Soon after that, he could no longer control his bowels and bladder, so he was dressed in large diapers. It took no keen, analytical thinking to realize that in a short time Jerry would be dead. He could only regress just so far.

One day, motivated by the desperateness of the situation, I sat down on the floor where Jerry was crawling around. I took his face in my hands and looked him straight in the eyes and said, "It's time to forgive yourself for taking acid. It's time to quit punishing yourself for blowing your mind. It's time to start living now." Over and over I repeated these words to Jerry while we sat on the floor of the hospital. I'm sure some of the nurses walking by were wondering if I had lost my mind; after all, Jerry was a vegetable now.

The next day he walked into group therapy, sat down on a couch, and began to talk. We were all amazed at his recovery. A nurse asked what had healed him and Jerry repeated what I had said to him the day before. The nurse asked him how many times he had repeated those words to himself. Jerry replied, "About ten to twenty thousand times."

I wonder how many people need to hear these healing words and repeat these words in order to be free of the destructive power of guilt:

> *It's time to forgive myself.*
> *It's time to quit punishing myself.*
> *It's time to start living now.*

I was twenty-eight years old before I made the decision to accept myself—all of me: the good stuff, the bad stuff, and the unknown stuff—all that is me I would accept as me, forgive myself, and love myself in case nobody else would love me. I realized as never before that my source of drivenness was to be accepted and loved by my father, and accepted and approved of by others in order to be healed of that certain funny feeling that I was not OK. So I made that decision to accept, forgive, and love myself as I am.

I also made an important decision to accept, forgive, and love my father and mother as they are, and not as I wanted them to be or how I felt they "should" have been.

God's Love Is Sufficient

I experienced God's love for me in a whole new light. I am loved by God because God is love and He accepts, forgives, and loves me even when I am messed up. I am loved because I need to be loved and not because I deserve God's love—I know I never can be good enough to deserve it. God forgives me because I need His love.

That day I was free of worrying about my earthly father's approval and my heavenly Father's approval. I was free to be me.

It was a liberating experience. It was as if previously I was the prisoner, and the jailer, too. The door to my prison cell was locked from the inside. Instead of waiting for someone else to set me free by unlocking the door, I discovered that I had the key to set myself free from my own private prison.

Having been healed of my drivenness for approval, I was able to discover another source of motivation, thanksgiving for what I had already received from God that I didn't deserve. The greatest gift from God was that He so loved Ken Olson that He gave His only Son to die on a cross for my sins and then be raised from the dead so I too would experience victory over death when Jesus returns.

Who Will Punch Your Ticket?

If you have ever gone skiing, you are familiar with the process of buying a ski-lift ticket and having a person punch your ticket so you can ride the ski lift all day.

In life, each of us has a ticket to be punched, the ticket of self-worth and self-approval. If you were raised with conditional love, then you will have a tendency to wait for someone else to punch your ticket and give you their stamp of approval. In an environment of conditional love, you always must earn and prove yourself worthy and good enough to be loved. But the trouble is that you never know when you have done enough to merit the approval you so desperately need.

When you find someone to punch your ticket, you feel good for a while, but soon that good feeling begins to weaken, and then you feel that you must submit another performance and approval ticket to be punched.

But what if you can't find anyone to punch your ticket? Or what if, when someone tries to punch your ticket, you reject it because you don't feel worthy enough or good enough inside to receive the good feeling of having your ticket punched? What then?

Then you begin to feel desperately depressed. You may even end up begging someone to punch your ticket, pleading with him and promising almost anything if only you can have your ticket punched.

Marriage can be the search for someone to punch your ticket. But what happens if your spouse also happens to be a person needing someone to punch his or her ticket? The waiting game begins, with each person waiting for the other to punch his or her ticket.

The truth is that God has already punched your ticket. No one else needs to do it. Now you need to love, own, forgive, and accept yourself even as God has already done.

Self-Acceptance Is a Dynamic Process

In my pilgrimage, I soon discovered that self-acceptance is not a static event. It is a dynamic process.

The self I accepted, loved, and forgave at twenty-eight is not the same person I am at fifty-six. That's because I am always growing and I am also outgrowing what I have been before.

Carl Rogers wrote these words on self-acceptance: "He who moves toward accepting all this changing complexity as a real part of himself—a crazy quilt variety of which he does not need to feel ashamed. He begins to own himself—a very precious possession. The more he owns himself, the more he can be himself."[2]

"To own oneself" is the decision to accept responsibility for one's life, choices, mistakes, emotional reactions, and to be responsible for your health or sickness.

It's so human, so tempting to turn over responsibility for your life to another person or government. Especially when you are hurting, confused, and floundering, you yearn for someone to take responsibility for your life and make everything all right again. I have learned to be very wary of a clever, charismatic man who, with deep, resonant voice makes it perfectly clear that "I've got it," and for several hundred dollars you can follow my teaching, and you will finally "get it."

Sheldon Kopp in his book, *If You Meet the Buddha on the Road, Kill Him!*, says, "The psychotherapy patient must also come to this heavy piece of understanding that he does not need the therapist. The most important things that each man must learn, no one else can teach him. Once he accepts this disappointment, he will be able to stop depending on the therapist, the guru, who turns out to be just another struggling human being. Illusions are hard, and it is painful to yield to this insight, that a grownup can be no man's disciple. This does not mark the end of the search, but a new beginning."[3] Sheldon Kopp is brilliant—he agrees with me!

No one can walk another person's pilgrimage, but one of the most liberating experiences is to know that you have permission to grow and change. As I gave the following poem I wrote as a gift to a friend, so too I would like to give you the gift of permission.

I HAVE PERMISSION

I have permission to break the chains
of yesterday's pain.
After all the strife,
A new lease on life.
I have permission at last
To be free,
To be me.
To throw away all the masks,
And stop those boring tasks.
I have permission
To trust,
To accept,
To love me.
I have permission to be the me
I was meant to be.
It's so strange how long it took
To look at me.
I'm not perfect,
But I'm not bad.
I can be sad,
    mad,
    glad,
    laugh and love.
Look out, world!
Since I have permission to love me,
There's so much love to give away.
The love of self and others
Is here to stay.[4]

CHECKPOINT

1. Think back to your childhood. What kind of personal feedback did you get in your home?

2. What were the factors that made your homelife healthy? What were the factors that made it unhealthy?

3. What is the relationship between being able to accept yourself and being able to accept what God has done for you?

4. What does it mean to "have your ticket punched"? How dependent are you on having it punched by others?

5. Sheldon Kopp wrote, "A grownup can be no man's disciple." In what sense do you agree and in what sense do you disagree?

THE
MAKING
OF A
MAN

part two

—2—
HOW
YOU
ARE
PROGRAMMED

Have you ever wondered how much your personality was shaped in the womb before you were born? I was conceived in the beginning of 1930. I was a depression pregnancy for a mother and father who already had two sons. I probably was not a wanted or planned pregnancy. Could this be when I received that "certain funny feeling that I was not OK"— when I was still in the womb?

One of my earliest memories was when I was four years old looking at pictures in a scrapbook at my maternal grandmother's home. There was a photograph of me just after I was brought home from the hospital. The next photograph was of my father, mother, and two brothers leaving for California in a Packard just after I was born. My mom's younger sister, Helen, took care of me while they were gone on that long trip from Omaha, Nebraska, to California. It always gave me a weird feeling, something like, "Here I am, and there goes the family to California."

We are finally beginning to study the workings of the human mind scientifically. It seems odd that we know much more about the moon and outer space than we do about the mind of man that is able to send people to the moon.

The memory bank of the mind is an incredible living computer. While a baby is in the womb, the memory bank begins to receive and store all kinds of information from the mother, the father, and events, and this affects the child in the womb. Thomas Verney, M.D., writes in his book *The Secret Life of the Unborn Child:* ". . . the unborn child is a feeling, remembering, aware being, and because he is, what happens to him—what happens to all of us—in the nine months between conception and birth—molds and shapes personality, drives, and ambitions in a very important way."[1]

Sources of Our Programming

The sources of significant programming naturally come first from the family and then from friends or enemies at school, teachers, peer groups, plus a constant influx of information from the various media. An important factor to remember is that it's not so much the single message that determines the course of a person's life, but the message that's repeated in many different ways throughout a person's life. As long as we live, we are receiving messages and making decisions about those messages. This is always making us change, alter, or reinforce our course in life.

The human brain isn't just a blank computer card on which the programming is punched. Our individual reactions to the messages we receive, and the resulting decisions about this information, are critical determinants in developing a person's belief system and his beliefs about the world in which he lives. In a way, the decisions begin to form from pictures of our own self-image and self-concept.

Unfortunately, a child receives a lot of information but lacks experience in living and can make some very bad decisions about the information he receives. These decisions become part of the foundation of his own personal belief system about himself and his world.

One woman recalled an incident that had been buried since she was five years old. She and a neighbor boy had been caught in some very normal exploration of each other's sexual plan when his mother caught them in the act. They were in the boy's garage. His mother screamed at her, "You're bad, you're bad." Now you have to picture this terrified five-year-old girl looking up at this enraged, screaming adult, and frantically trying to find out what she had done that was bad enough to have a woman scream at her so violently. Surely it couldn't be harmlessly looking at each other's bodies? She made a decision. There wasn't anything she had done that was that bad, but it must mean that she was bad. I asked her what she did with her tears when she went home. She couldn't let mom or dad see her tears because then they would ask questions. She said, "I stopped my tears before I went home." She made another decision to the effect that she would never let her emotions show too much, because someone might discover the greatest fear—that she was bad. She began to believe and then live a life of no love and developed a self-image that she wasn't good enough. She held people off so they would never discover her awful secret.

Other times, this programming is much more subtle. A child is told over and over in many ways what a brilliant older brother or sister he has, but the parents love him just as much as they do the older brother or sister. The child realizes that he will never receive all the attention the older sibling receives. He doesn't feel that he ever can, so he doesn't try.

The parents reinforce this by saying, "We don't expect that much from you."

The child begins to internalize that his parents don't expect much from him, so maybe there isn't much to do. Thus, he doesn't expect much from himself. I doubt if any father would knowingly say this directly to his son: "Now listen to me, son. When you grow up, I want you to be the most insecure and fear-ridden man alive. Don't you ever expect anything good in life such as success or happiness, because you are a nothing, son, a *big fat zero!*" If a child heard that blunt message, he would probably react by thinking, "Dad, you are really messed up. You ought to see someone about your problem. You need help."

As extreme as this illustration is, the truth is that many children grow into adulthood firmly believing that they are big fat zeros and they are riddled with fear and insecurity. They believe that they're no good and that the "no-goods" of life is what they should deserve and expect. They were so subtly programmed that they began to believe this and live accordingly.

Just for fun, try to discover a little of the programming you received as a child. What messages did you receive concerning the following topics? (You must remember that a large amount of the programming was nonverbal, based on your observations of the interactions of your parents and others in the family.) How were you programmed about conditional or unconditional love? What value did work have in your family? Achievement, play, sex, intimacy, money, discipline, expressing human emotions such as anger, love, and violence, feelings about being a man or woman? There are many other topics that you could list, but I'm sure that you get some idea that you are programmed far more deeply than you are aware. And that some of your earliest fears and unhappy experiences affected you and you made a decision about them.

Family Communication Patterns

Also, take a look at the family communication system. Families have communication patterns and rules about what is allowed to be talked about and what is taboo. In your family how was guilt used to manipulate and control people? Families can even develop their own myths of greatness: "We're all one great big happy family, and don't you ever speak to the contrary, it's forbidden." "Don't ever rock the boat." "We are a peaceful family; peace at any price." There is also some family cultural programming that is passed on from one generation to another, based upon how people should behave because of their cultural heritage. There is also a uniqueness factor operating in families. So often we neglect the fact that each individual is unique, as unique as your thumbprint is a unique statement of your uniqueness. In some dysfunctional families, a person's uniqueness or differentness is labeled as bad or threatening to the family unit. In some families a child dare not be different, and in the extreme case a child dare not be, period.

Each person is born with his own genetic coding. I know the next time around I'd like to find some genes that wouldn't give me premature baldness! We also enter the world with a unique neurological system which operates at its own unique rate. If you doubt me, just talk to a parent who's had a hyperactive child on how their neurological rate of activity affected their feelings about the child.

The family unit is always in a state of change. The first shock on the family system is the arrival of the first child. Remember there is only one first child in a family, one second child, one third child, and so on. With each child born in the family, there is a change in family relationships. The wife can become overinvolved with the birth of the first child, and the husband, and now father, can feel somewhat pushed aside— so he may put more energy into his work and his outside activities. The arrival of the second child may not be appreciated by the first child who has now been removed from the center stage of the family. Thus, the new arrival isn't always welcomed by some family members.

Boys Need Role Models

Family programming can also include the development of family roles for each of the children. The children will live out these programmed roles in the family. There can be the family brain, the living doll, the family clown, the loser, the rebel, the black sheep. The family programming can also include the roles or careers the child shall choose such as the family priest, the doctor, or lawyer.

Many years ago, our country was predominantly rural. A boy could grow up on the farm and see how and what his father did for a living. How he acted and reacted. Thus, he had a very clear and concise role model as to what was a man. Very often the father became an idol for the boy to admire and to imitate. The boy would even adopt some of his father's mannerisms of walk and pretend that he was smoking a corn-cob pipe just like daddy did. They would work hour after hour together and they would also talk about the world in which they lived. But this world changed when America became an urban country. Dad left in the morning to go somewhere to work, do something, and then he returned at night, tired, maybe even after the children were asleep. The boy didn't know what his father did. They no longer spent the hours together. A boy needs an idol, and when the father isn't there, or is too vague, he looks for another man to be his idol. But, where have all the idols gone?

In working with hard-core delinquent boys, I've always been struck with the absence of idols, adults that they look up to as role models. In the drug culture there were idols, but they were acid-rock stars, which were, in my opinion, negative role models. Such role models as Jimi Hendrix, Jim Morrison, and Janis Joplin. We also went through a period of debunking idols in history. So it was not acceptable to have a traditional idol from the past. The age of cynicism and despair left little room for idols and role models.

I fortunately grew up in a time when it was permissible to have idols. I had idols like Booker T. Washington, Cole Porter, Joe Louis, Tony Zale, the legendary Four Horsemen of Notre Dame, James Cagney, football players like Johnny Lujack, and many more. But then I had many others in real life who made an important impact upon my life.

When I was a boy, my older brother George, who was six years older than I, was a powerful influence on me. George had quite an active imagination. At night he would tell my brother Stan and me stories of when he was fighting the Boer War in Africa. At times he would tell us of his expeditions with Roy Chapman Andrews as they explored the Gobi desert in Mongolia searching for the remains of dinosaurs. Naturally by the time I was ten, one of the first books I read was *Exploring with Andrews*. Other nights he would tell us tales of Genghis Khan. He would also recite poetry like Kipling's "Gunga Din," Robert Service's "The Shooting of Dan McGrew" and "The Cremation of Sam McGee." I admit that those aren't the great classics of all time, but they are my favorites. I can't tell you what an emotional thrill it was a few years ago to be able to see the famous Malamute saloon in Alaska. I could almost hear my brother George's voice reciting the tale of "The Shooting of Dan McGrew." I've also been blessed with important men who served as idols for me. When I was a teenager, my pastor was a hero for me as he was for many others. He had done everything in life, plus he was a gifted storyteller. I owe much to two brothers who were my father's business partners. They treated me like a son. My football coach in high school and my first boss both enriched me by treating me as someone who was real. A boy needs idols, role models, real men to help him become a man.

For a growing boy, there is nothing like a man to show him the way to manhood.

CHECKPOINT

1. What were the circumstances of your birth? Do you think those circumstances have affected you?

2. Are you a first child, second child, or third child? Has the birth order of your siblings programmed your life?

3. Who were your role models as you grew up? In sports? In entertainment? In your community? In your extended family? In literature? In history? How have they shaped your thinking about manhood?

—3—

THE DEVELOPMENT OF MASCULINITY

How many men ever take the time and energy to examine the inner workings that make us tick? I have found it to be difficult for a man to be open or introspective with another person. It's too simplistic to think that a man's just afraid to look at himself to any degree of depth. Perhaps he doesn't think it's necessary. How often does a man deal with another man, openly revealing himself? I have noticed that a married man is very reluctant to talk to another person about his wife with any degree of intimacy. With divorced men, well, that's a different cup of tea. It has been rumored that divorced men are prone to conduct postmortems on their former wives, especially in the company of another woman.

The Formative Years

What are some of the events or memories that stand out in a boy's formative years that will be instrumental in developing his self-concept and decisions about his masculinity? Every man will have his own unique story to tell which will contain pertinent memories, decisions, values, beliefs, and the programming from his parents. What makes Johnny run so hard and die so young? Is it that so many men are programmed to live with the killing pressure of perfectionism as one of the qualifications in developing masculinity?

In discussing his personal programming, a dentist stated that his mother gave the instruction, "Be perfect." From his father the instruction was, "Be a dentist." In combination he was instructed to be a "perfect dentist." His family chestnut was, "Idle hands are the devil's workshop."

Here is how the instruction had affected his life. When I met Johnny at a seminar, he was fifty-six years old, brilliant, and an excellent, highly respected dentist. He started every Monday with an excruciating migraine that would not lessen in pain until he vomited. Then he was ready to go to the office and see patients.

John liked being a dentist, but he was in conflicting rebellion against the programming to "be perfect" and to "be a dentist." John began to examine his decision to be a dentist, without reference to his father's instruction to be a dentist, and he decided that in spite of his father, he liked being a dentist.

I know this sounds weird to some of you, but I gave John permission not to be perfect. To believe that he was a beautiful person, but he could never be perfect. I gave him permission to stop striving to be a perfect dentist and accept the goal of being an excellent dentist, which he already was at the time.

Later in the afternoon John confided that for some reason he was experiencing anger toward me. He didn't know why. I suggested that maybe his parents' past instructions were angry at me for giving him permission to be free of their power in his life.

A week after the seminar he wrote me to report on the great sense of relief he was experiencing with his life. There were no more migraine headaches. He could look forward to going to the office because he didn't have to prove to himself thirty-six times a day that he was a good dentist. He could admit that he was an excellent dentist, but he no longer had to try to be a perfect dentist.

His family chestnut of "idle hands are the devil's workshop" had made him guilty even thinking of recreation, but he gave the child in him permission to take up sailing for fun. Now he is an avid sailor.

The Pressure of Perfectionism

The pressure of perfectionism is a killer. It has always amazed me how imperfect parents, with their normal share of hang-ups, can insist that their children be perfect. Maybe they believe that producing a perfect child proves to the world that they were good parents. The programming for perfection sounds so noble and righteous, but it produces such miserable people.

The destructive tape of perfectionism means that once you have made a mistake, you are not perfect; but is that the end of it? No—a person is instructed to try harder next time. Ironically, even though a person tries harder next time, it's never good enough. Someone is always pointing out a flaw, saying, "You could have done it better."

A male perfectionist is driven to be ambitious, to achieve, earn good grades, or other visual merit badges. Driven men do accomplish a great deal. When a boy becomes a man, he can decorate the walls of his den with his service plaques and cups of appreciation. Such a perfectionist is a goal setter, but the goals are only the means to reach his "impossible dream."

This type of man is a mountain climber with his goals. He believes that if he sets this goal and reaches it, then he will be happy. The goal could be financial, the purchase of a prized object, or public recognition. So full steam ahead he charges up this mountain, dashing by people who are going at a slower pace or who may have even stopped. He shakes his head in disgust and races ever upward. Finally he makes it to the top of the mountain, breathing very hard. Then it hits him, "I made it to the top, so why don't I feel great and exuberant about reaching this goal? Why do I feel let down?"

Then he looks from the mountaintop and sees another mountain to climb. So without even savoring his achievement, or giving himself credit for making it to the top, or resting to absorb the beautiful view, he retreats down that mountain to find another mountain to climb. His deep desire is the hope that this next goal will provide him with the inner psychological payoff be so desperately needs.

The tragic part of the driven perfectionist is that the payoff never happens. The reason is that a man is programmed to be perfect by his parents, thus when he achieves a significant goal or accomplishment, the parents receive the credit for being such good parents and motivating their son. The achiever only gets credit for finally obeying his parents' instructions and doing what he's been told. This is a reason why goals and achievements fail to provide the psychological payoff for the perfectionist and why he's robbed of enjoying his pride in accomplishment. He hasn't learned to punch his own ticket.

A perfectionist is also a brittle person who thinks only in black or white. There's no tolerance for any shade of gray. Something is either right or wrong, usually meaning my way or the wrong way. If challenged to defend the self-defeating drive, the perfectionist will often respond, "So you want me to be a slob, to just sit back and be a bum?"

To live or work with a perfectionist can be a wearing task. The perfectionist demands perfection from those around him. There's no way you can please him. The inner dialogue of a perfectionist reveals the dirty words of *should, ought, would,* and *could.* These are words of psychological tyranny. I should be perfect—you should be perfect, they ought to be perfect, ad nauseam. A perfectionist would be able to relax and join the human race if he could eliminate those dirty words from his thoughts and speech. A perfectionist needs to put a stop sign in his bathroom or at his office. The stop sign would read: "I will not 'should' on myself today."

A perfectionist can change, but it's a painful process for the man as well as those who suffer with the man. First of all, it's programmed so deeply and has become such habitual behavior that to conceive of thinking and responding any other way is difficult—because "That's the way I am." Also a perfectionist seldom believes or admits that there's anything wrong with him. It's other people, the rest of the world, they're the ones who "should" change. There's a fear of change that's rooted in the programming from the significant others in his life, which results in a man being unable to trust his own thinking, feelings, and decisions. It then becomes a shaky experience to make a leap of faith to trust and believe in oneself. It's foreign for a perfectionist to believe that motivation can be derived from trusting himself. He can't see himself still being productive when not driven by perfectionism. It's so hard to conceive, much less believe.

After a discussion on perfectionism in a seminar, a mother reported back to the group after lunch that all of a sudden it hit her that she had been asking and expecting her ten-year-old son to be perfect. During lunch she confessed to me that she had been wrong, and now he would have her permission not to be perfect. He could just be himself and do the best he could. Later she said that when she told her son this, he just stared at her in stunned amazement. Then he asked if she meant what she said. She said yes. Then he jumped up and down and around the bedroom gleefully shouting, "Yippee, yippee."

Perfectionism is just one of the many pressures a man may experience in developing his concept of masculinity. This makes it very difficult for a man to admit he's made a mistake. It seems that someone is always holding a carrot out in front of us, just out of reach, and we are to be motivated to chase the carrot the rest of our lives. I wonder how many men spend a lifetime chasing carrots and never stop long enough to ask, "Do I even like carrots?"

The Pressure to Achieve

I don't know when I was seduced into the pressure to achieve in school. My parents didn't stress good grades or push to pursue higher education. Yet somewhere I picked up the pressure tape to do well in school. Along with the tape to be a good student was the peer pressure to be a "tough guy." Thus, I had to be careful not to do too well in school. Maybe the striving was just another carry-over from my basic need for approval and acceptance. I always looked up to the brains in the class and secretly wished I could be a "brain," but my self-confidence was too shaky for that goal, and besides, I wasn't a star in mathematics. I did learn, however, to solve the problem of going to school and winning. I have completed twelve years of college and graduate schools, but I still have a recurring dream that I'm in school, close to final week, and I suddenly remember I haven't attended one of the courses I am enrolled in, so I know I will fail.

I loved football from my first exposure to the game, playing with my older brothers and their friends when I was six years old. The first time I played I was given the ball and ran for a touchdown. There was only one thing wrong: I ran the wrong way! At six years of age it seemed so logical. The other way was filled with bigger kids.

We moved many times when I was growing up. I went to ten grammar schools in eight years. I used athletics to win people's approval. I pushed myself hard in football so I could make some friends before the next move. I played hard, but I was never the best athlete. In my class I always envied the natural athletes.

When I was eleven I experienced a growth spurt. With that growth came that clumsy stage. I would trip over my shoe-string and fall down. We had, at this time, moved from Houston, Texas, to Mesa, Arizona, for my brother Stan's health. At fifteen he was only four feet nine inches tall and weighed sixty-seven pounds. But since he was four years older than I and nimble and quick, he spent hour after hour with a football running at me, faking me out. I fell repeatedly, clutching the air and hitting that hard adobe soil. He knew how much football meant to me. My feet were growing so fast that my older brother George wanted to give my shoes to the navy for gunboats after all the ships were sunk at Pearl Harbor. Consequently I picked up the new nickname—"Gunboat"—and the belief that I was clumsy.

The belief in my clumsy behavior was next evident as a teenage boy learning to dance. I'll never forget the girl who informed me that I had no sense of rhythm. Now that doesn't help one become a dancer. "Old Clumsy with no sense of rhythm."

Proving Oneself a Man

I had the feeling that growing up from a boy to a man was nothing but a long obstacle course that demanded you prove yourself a man. It was accepted as normal for boys to be aggressive and competitive, while girls were to be good little girls who were eager to please others.

We lived at one point in a section of Houston called Park Place, right next door to Harrisberg and the tough "channel rats." My two older brothers, who were slight of build and short, decided that since I was the "big one" of the litter, I should learn how to box. It was a good thing because I was a nice-looking boy with straw blond hair and blue eyes. Other boys were always trying to make my eyes black and blue. At ten I quickly discovered I had to prove myself tough on the average of at least once a week. It was always on my mind when I went to school. Who will it be today that I will have to fight? I lived up to my initials, K.O., and I became very good with my fists. In fact, I never lost a fight. I became so good I began to look for kids to beat up.

I don't like to share this side of me with you, but I have had to come to terms with the violence in me. I can't blame it all on Houston.

As I look back on the intensity of the way I played football in high school and college, it scares me. I wasn't just aggressive, I was mean. I wanted to hurt people. Evidently it was accepted or approved by the adults around me. I was caught up in proving my masculinity by being a tough guy. Snapshots of me when I was a teenager reveal how I tried to scowl to create a tough appearance. In looking at old newspaper clippings of me about to make a tackle, my teeth were clenched and my face was twisted in violence. I even gave some serious thought to becoming a professional boxer. Naturally my idols were all boxers and football players.

Something happened in my senior year of high school that initiated a change in my violent behavior. One Sunday evening after a church youth meeting, a bunch of us went to the Eneanto Park clubhouse to dance. As we walked into the clubhouse a fistfight was in progress. A big fellow was beating up on a younger, smaller boy. I stopped the fight and said to the bigger man, "Cut it out. This isn't a fair fight." Well, this man did not appreciate my stopping his beating on the little guy, so he hit me. He was drunk and I soon knocked him across the room. He was out on his feet, leaning against the wall. Then, in that split second, I made a decision that was a turning point in my violent behavior. I could have gone on and given this man a beating. Then this thought hit me. "You could kill this guy with your fists." I stopped and told his buddy to get himself and his friend out of there, quickly! "I could have killed him" was a chilling revelation.

I still hadn't come to terms with the depths of violence in me. When our first son, Mike, was five years old (oh, how I hate to admit this) he was on a TV boxing show from Los Angeles called "Kid Gloves." Mike had all the natural talent athletically that I had always dreamed about. I had started boxing classes for kids five to fourteen years of age in our church in Canoga Park. I was kidded about being a "punchy parson." I went to a match with Mike, dressed in my clerical garb, complete with that horrible stiff white clerical collar. After the bout, a man walked over to me and what he related shook me to the core. He said, "I watched your face as your son boxed tonight, and you are the most violent man I have ever seen."

That judgment was a devastating blow to me and my self-image. It shook me deeply, but only recently have I been able to examine and even accept the violence in me. Where the violence came from I don't know, but I have to admit it's there. I believe that I have it under control; although I still have some violent fantasies, I have changed my violence potential.

I was raised with guns, the out-of-doors, and hunting. Now I don't even own a gun, nor do I hunt.

I even passed an unexpected test of my ability to control my violence. A couple of summers ago our church slow-pitch softball team was playing a practice game with another team. Their pitcher was a violent person. He purposefully crashed into our catcher and broke his collar bone. Then he dared our pastor to crash into him as he blocked home plate. Now remember, this was only a practice game. I came around to score a run and this pitcher was standing with the catcher blocking home plate. Now I have to admit I was thinking, *should I deck them both for hurting our catcher? No,* I said to myself, *it's just a softball game. Touch home plate and don't hurt anyone.* I stepped on home plate and just brushed against the two players. Suddenly I heard a scream and this pitcher came running at me and gave me a karate kick at my face. He missed, hitting my shoulder, and his baseball cleats tore it open. He was a little guy and I didn't go after him because I heard the sentence, *You could kill him with your hands.* It took six men to hold my son Mike from getting at him, and it was a good thing; for I saw the same violence in his eyes that night, and he could have killed him.

It's painful for me to be this honest with you. I would like to only share with you what a nice guy I am. What a kind and tender person I am. But the truth is, I am both violent *and* tender and kind.

The Problem of Violence

I'm concerned with the blatant abuse of television and movies for showing so much violent behavior. To be sure, it isn't an easy subject to conduct research on the effects of television and movies on viewers' behavior. There are those who believe the media isn't harmful to viewers because everyone knows it's just a film and filled with fantasy. What disturbs me is that people's minds are being programmed to become more violent. Pictures of violence are recorded on the memory banks of the mind, and if the pictures are repeated often enough, it becomes a deeply accepted imprint. Violence is exhibited by the behavior of the police as well as criminals on such shows, and the conclusion is that violence is a way of life.

There are emerging statistics concerning the alarming increase of violent crimes by young people showing that certain films portraying crimes of violence do produce an increase in such crimes. It still shakes me when I think of the young people I have had in therapy who committed murder, and how unaffected they were by what they have done.

"Why did you kill that person?" I have asked, only to receive a shrug of the shoulders and a reply—"He was in my way," or "Someone said he was a snitch."

"Would you do it again?"—"Yes."

Many of the public schools in our society are filled with violent young people, armed with knives and guns. Believe it or not, in some schools it's a raw act of courage to go to the bathroom because you never know when you will be knifed or beaten. I was once asked by a mother on a radio talk show what I would suggest she do because her son was afraid to go to school. I asked what happened at school. "My son got stabbed." In some cities, being a teacher is a more dangerous job than being a policeman or fireman.

I believe that one of the reasons for the increase in violent crimes is the programming of people to violence. Even the news media appears to feel that violent news is the best news. I wonder when we are going to begin to come to terms with the violence in our movies, television shows, pro sports, or in each of us.

Is Competition a Character Builder?

They say competition is a character builder in helping a boy to become a successful man. Competition is as American as apple pie and the flag. The Lombardi credo is prevalent across the land. "Winning isn't everything, it's the only thing." Competition is pressure to pit oneself against another. It teaches life by comparisons and one-upmanship. A person can only win by making the other person look bad. Competition breeds anxiety, loneliness, and distrust of others.

When a boy enters school he is expected to beat the others in a race. He must be Number One. That's life by the numbers, by the scores, or the grades. Our daughter Jan was told that if she read a hundred books while in the first grade she would be in the Book Worm Club. Jan read a hundred books. That was the goal. Somehow something was lost in the numbers game. She made it to the magic number, but she never discovered the joy of reading.

If the goal is to memorize a list of words for spelling, a child can get a hundred. The goal is just to memorize, not learn or understand the meaning of the words. After the test, the words can be forgotten.

Report cards become so important for parents and children as a measuring stick of how well, or poorly, they do in comparison to other children. This pressure for numbers has caused an imbalance in the purpose of education. I'm naive enough to believe that education should draw out the uniqueness in each of us, help us think, be curious, and develop skills in problem behavior.

I asked my son Danny who had always loved to think, fantasize, and create games, how he liked going to college. I will never forget his response: "Dad, they don't want you to think." He's now applying to medical schools but still says, "Dad, it's the same numbers game again, only with intense pressure."

Education went through a convulsive spasm when the Russians successfully launched their first Sputnik. Horror of horrors, the Russians were ahead of us in our race to outer space. It was a national disgrace to be second. Naturally public education was the scapegoat. How could our school systems fail us so long? As a result, intense pressure was placed on public instruction. As a nation we had to mass-produce experts in science and mathematics. Mathematics that was previously taught in the eighth grade was shoved down the throats of fifth graders. It was as if every young boy had to be either an engineer or scientist. Our oldest son was exposed to three totally different courses in modern math in three years. All it did was create confusion and defeat in Mike. When Mike was twenty-two, I asked if he could remember when he felt the pressure to be a man. He replied, "I was in the fifth grade. All of a sudden it hit me. I realized the pressure and felt the responsibility that I had to make it as a man."

I have seen the compulsion to win humiliate boys in Little League baseball—young boys ridiculed for dropping a fly ball, or striking out, or making an error. I was a Little League pitching coach for a while so I have seen the inevitable destruction. After one game, when a player had made a spectacular catch in center field to end the game and preserve the victory, I heard his mother say, "It's a good thing you caught that ball or you would have been in trouble." I couldn't stand it, so I said, "Ma'am, you forget he caught the ball. Even if he hadn't caught the ball, it would have been all right because he sure did try. Even major league ball players are human enough to make errors. Should we demand a higher level of excellence for these kids playing ball?"

Kids used to have fun playing ball, until parents organized them and took the fun away with competitive pressure. Whether it's Pop Warner football or the latest craze— "Tennis anyone?"—are we putting too much pressure on our kids?

I wonder how many young boys who don't have the physical size, coordination, or interest in sports are made to feel less of a boy by a father who pressures him to go out for sports anyway. Dad's disapproval of not having a star athlete for a son can crush the spirit in his son. No son likes to feel he's a big disappointment to his father. To protect himself and his shaky, devastated self-concept, this boy can build a wall around himself, withdraw from life, and he'll feel the pain of loneliness. He can also constantly berate himself for not measuring up to the other boys or, more importantly, his father's dreams. This self-doubt can cause him to put down his masculinity and cast a cloud of guilty gloom over his whole life.

The pressure to compete against one another leads a man to ploys of power so he can defeat or be compared more favorably to someone else. It's not a great discovery that a man can usually find someone less able or talented than himself, but too often a man competes against another, wins, and then stops growing. The basic challenge for each man is to discover his potential, then set his own goals for his life's growth. This need to play games of one-upmanship helps men develop big ego problems.

Ego-Tripping

As a boy grows up, he feels the need to prove that he is better than someone else. I wonder if the comparison game is where the need to lie and cheat begins. I know that when I was in high school, boys would brag and boast of being great "studs." In my senior year of high school I was the constant butt of jokes by my fellow football players because I was still a virgin. When I dated a new girl, the rumors would be spread that I had finally fallen. There would be more teasing, more fantastic stories by some other football player bragging about his sexual powers and latest conquest. As I look back on those years, I think we could have named the group "The Liars Club."

One summer, when I was working in a filling station while attending college summer school, a shy young Mexican man endured a hazing before his marriage. The other men tormented him daily with sexual jokes and their own personal sexual powers. Finally, Manuel got married and went on a honeymoon. When he returned to work, all the men gathered around to hear about his wedding night. First, each man told exaggerated tales of how many times he had intercourse with his wife on his wedding night. The next man embellished his story to top the previous man's account until finally all the braggers were finished. Someone asked Manuel, "Well, Manuel, how many times did you and your wife have intercourse on your wedding night?"

"Only once," replied Manuel shyly.

"Only once?" shouted the group of men in chorus.

"Yes," replied Manuel, "only once. You see, we weren't used to it."

I'm afraid a man turns off a woman by his constant need to impress her with what a big man he was, is, or can be with her. I thought as a young man that women were attracted to a man's physique. As a result, I worked out in college to develop the muscle-man look. Only after I was married did Jeannie have the courage to tell me that she wasn't impressed with my muscles, but my personality.

A man's need to talk about himself makes for a bored woman who feels she must tolerate his ego trip. Franklin P. Jones once said, "One way for a woman to get a man's complete attention is by listening to him."

What's behind this hot-air facade and ego-tripping is an attempt to puff up my ego so you won't see how insecure I am behind my plastic mask. If I don't impress you about how great I am, you will never like or appreciate me. After all, he that tooteth not his own horn has it not tooted at all. I'm aware that when I feel insecure inside, that's when I become like a blowfish that puffs himself up with air. This is also a psychological hazard for men who make a living as platform speakers, entertainers, or public personalities. The heat of the spotlight tends to melt brains a little. Men, including me, suffer from delusions of grandeur. They also tend to get excited about life and what they're doing. Consequently they can't wait to tell others, whether they want to hear about it or not.

I must confess that being an author is an ego trip. There's

an old story about an author at a cocktail party who trapped a group of people, then talked and talked about his first book to the "captive audience." After an hour of boring the people to death, he suddenly said, "Enough of my talking about myself, it's your turn to talk. What did you think of my latest book?" Once in a while I have been as bad, and as tedious. Fortunately, I have a wife who is helping me take the cure for that problem.

The pressures of perfect performance and competition create a basic anxiety in man to hide his weaknesses, emotions, and fears, for if he doesn't, others might believe that his masculine mystique is only a masculine mistake. Deep down the fear of failure and rejection haunts and drives a man to be aggressive, to play his games of "let's pretend," and to reinforce his need to look good by putting down other people.

CHECKPOINT

1. On a scale of one to ten, where do you place yourself as a perfectionist?

2. What is the relationship between perfectionism and masculinity?

3. What are the dangers in perfectionism?

4. How important is aggressiveness in your view of masculinity? Should it be more important or should it be less important?

5. Imagine that you are the coach of a Little League baseball team. What kind of pep talk do you give to the team before the big game?

6. How important is sexual prowess in your view of masculinity?

7. Competitive pressures create a tendency in men to hide weaknesses, emotions, and fears. What are you hiding?

—4—

IT'S SO
HARD
TO
CRY

It's so hard for a man to cry,
Even when I try, the tear ducts are dry.
Bloodshot eyes reveal the pain.
But—be brave—be strong—is how I've
Been trained.
Keep a stiff upper lip.
Be careful not to slip
And let a teardrop fall.
A man must always stand tall.
No one knows when I'm scared or weak.
Only with ulcers can I weep.
Hardening arteries from a heart grown cold,
Deprived of tenderness, softness, and love,
I feel very old.
I feel! Is that what I said?
Maybe I can cry before I'm dead.

The tears are so warm and real.
I'm finally alive and able to feel,
A man of flesh and not of steel.

As I wrote that poem, it recalled a drawing of a man given to me by an artistic teenager in a children's psychiatric ward of a state hospital. It was a side view of a man's head with no hair. It looked like a mannequin. A portion of the skull was removed, but instead of seeing the brain you saw parts of a machine made of steel. The only evidence of humanness was a tear beginning its journey from the eye down the cheek.

At least not being able to cry isn't one of my problems. I cry when I'm happy or when I'm sad, whenever strong emotions are awakened in me. When I watched the father discover his children singing "the hills are alive with the sound of music" in the movie *The Sound of Music,* well, I was overcome with emotion and tears. I'm not even discreet, nor do I try to disguise the fact that my nose is running. When I blow my nose, it sounds like the honking of a wild goose. Movies like *Brian's Song,* where two men are able to express their love and friendship for each other, get to me. My wife and children have seen me cry. They know I'm not ashamed to cry. There were times, when I was working with kids who were using drugs, that their destructiveness and my limitations caused me pain. Often I refused to read the daily paper for fear one of the kids I knew had been arrested, died of an overdose, committed suicide, been murdered, or committed murder. Sometimes when I would have an open hour in my schedule, I would close the drapes, turn off the lights, and let go of the pain inside through my tears. I know this doesn't sound very professional, but when I cry I know that I'm still alive.

The "cool" man is very macho, aloof, and always in control of his emotions. This image is portrayed as *the* role model for a man. I feel sorry for a "cool" man whose emotions are cold and who, of necessity, must hide behind a mask to be real. I fear he's seldom real.

Why Are We Afraid of Our Feelings?

Many men are afraid to feel, to become aware of their deep emotions, longings, and dreams. Have you ever asked a man how he *felt* about something, and then noticed that when he responded, he said what he thought not what he felt? It's sad to watch a man struggle and flounder when he's asked again to report how he feels; and then so often he'll respond in bewilderment, "I—I don't know how to feel, much less know what I feel."

There are at least two emotions that a man has permission to express—anger and sexuality. This same man who doesn't know how to describe his feelings may be transformed into a raving maniac over a football game or other sporting event. Secretly many a wife wishes that her man would carry over some of this emotional enthusiasm to their marriage.

"Men don't cry" is an old cliché, but have you ever wondered why a little boy or a grown man isn't supposed to cry? The usual answer is that boys and men aren't supposed to cry because that shows weakness. After all, boys and men are programmed to be strong. This answer sounds so reasonable and true, but what's the purpose behind a man not crying? For whose benefit is it that a boy or man doesn't cry?

Here is what I discovered as a possible answer. If a man cries, a behavior pattern which has been so often labeled as weakness, it will threaten a wife's security.

"If my man is weak, who will be strong for me and take care of me?" Think about it for a minute. A woman is programmed from childhood to be a sweet, nice little girl. A man will provide her with financial and emotional security. A woman's programming is often of the nature that "there's nothing like a man to make her feel safe and secure." So maybe it's a woman who puts the plugs in the tear ducts of a man. Remember, I said this may be one answer, not necessarily *the* answer.

There are other possible considerations, such as cultural programming, which fluctuates in giving men permission to cry and express emotions. I have even thought that the climate is related to people's emotional expressiveness. I have noted that cold climates seem to produce emotionally cold people, whereas the warmer the climate, the warmer the emotional responsiveness. Maybe all that some "cold Swedes" need is to move to the South Pacific for a while, so they can defrost emotionally and warm up as human beings. (I pick on the Swedes since that is my heritage.)

What Are We Hiding?

If a man has difficulty in getting in touch with his emotions, then what happens to basic emotions and reactions? They are denied, repressed, shoved aside, but the energy of them can't be denied or repressed. Emotions still remain and demand expression in some manner.

Instead of girl watching, try watching men. Look at their faces lined with taut frown muscles and clenched teeth. A man's walk will often reveal the load he is carrying on his back. His rapid pace may reveal the strain of living with stress and deadlines. Study a man smoking a cigarette. Is the cigarette relaxing him or is he nervous? Does a chain-smoker's puffing give a clue to a need to let off steam? A man gulping his first cocktail and quickly ordering another one: Is this how he numbs the pain and ache for a while? The way a man can swallow one bit of food after another, without tasting or enjoying his meal, makes a person wonder what he is trying to swallow emotionally, hoping he won't choke. "When I suppress an emotion my stomach keeps score—one—two—three—four."[1]

A man can only fool himself, denying and suppressing his emotions, for just so long. In time there will be tissue damage, heart attacks, ulcers, depression, and someday he may blow up in violence directed at his wife, children, or even himself by putting the cold barrel of a pistol in his mouth and blowing his brains out. Then he feels no pain, no tension or distress. Peace at last.

Our everyday language is filled with words and phrases that are indicative of the programming of man not to show his emotions. Men are told to bottle up emotions, keep 'em under control. Get a hold of yourself. Get a grip on yourself. Don't fall to pieces—ad infinitum.

An English teacher once did some research, and she came up with some 340 expressions in the English language that mean "get tight" for control.

From a cognitive point of view, men are programmed to be thinkers and problem solvers, to be analytical, scientific, and objective. In the scientific, technical, mechanical world we live in, these qualities have been absolutely vital. When an engineer designs a bridge, you want to know how strong it will be and how long it will last. It isn't too important to know how the engineer "feels" about the bridge, because that doesn't answer the question that needs to be answered. The world of science and technology demands accuracy and people who can be precise.

The scientific method of thinking and reasoning is a need in some areas of life, but it should not exclude the awareness of emotions, intuitions, empathy, and subjectivity. Someday I'm going to write a book about how to be married to an engineer. After listening to engineers and their wives in counseling, I see the frustrations of wives living with men who are dense, insensitive, and unaware of what it takes to satisfy a wife's emotional needs. One wife said, "If I ask my husband how much do you love me, he will probably reach for his slide rule, do some calculating, and say, 'Oh about this much.' "

Unfortunately, however, relationship problems are not solved with the logical deductive reasoning process of A + B = C.

When a man becomes primarily a logical-deductive reasoner, he becomes emotionally constipated and unaware of the subjective side of life. This can result in the inability of a man to experience empathy for another person or to experience the other person's world of reality. How many wives plead with their husbands, "Don't just hear the words, but please listen to me. Feel my frustration and pain, and don't shut me out. Please don't react to me as if I am a machine."

I once heard a man in a calm, emotionless voice tell me that he had just discovered his wife was having an affair with another man. I asked him how he felt about this discovery. His reply caused me to break out in a cold sweat. "Oh, I don't feel anything, one way or the other. I don't hate my wife, or the other man. I think I'll get my pistol and kill them both." I knew this man had a high potential for violence. A few years earlier he almost killed a man with a hammer during an argument at work. I don't think I ever worked so hard to get a man to break down and pour forth the violent emotions he was denying. Thankfully, he didn't solve his marriage problem with violence.

The Price of Being Safe

What else is there that causes so many men to be emotionally constipated? A young boy quickly discovers that if he shows emotions like crying, or being too sensitive, he is called a sissy and is warned not to be "like a girl." A girl can be a tomboy, but who ever heard of a janeboy? In his exposure to the cruelties of his world, a young boy learns to develop protective armor so he won't be easily hurt. People won't know when he is weak or vulnerable. There can be a deep fear in a man that if he opens the secret door to his heart, you will see the unvarnished, unmasked real male, with all the insecurities and fears. When he is unprotected and vulnerable you will hurt him and use his weakness against him. You may be repulsed by what you see in him, and then you will reject him or even laugh at him.

Maybe this fear and memories of experiences when he was hurt by being open and vulnerable cause him to make the decision, "I'll never let anyone get that close to me again." So he develops this suit of armor to protect himself.

The price he pays for being safe inside his suit of armor is loneliness, because other people will be unable to share his fears, his hurts, or his dreams. Loneliness is believed better than risking oneself to openness—for when you are in the open, people take pot shots at you. I've known a few men who have their armor plate so perfected, that no matter how long you've known them or tried to get inside, you have concluded that you will never know them. The suit of armor works. It does keep a man protected from other people, but it also prevents the man inside from breaking out of his deep loneliness, prevents him from experiencing love—deep feelings, awareness, and aliveness. He is like the Tin Man in the immortal *Wizard of Oz*, whose song is "If I Only Had a Heart." If you could look inside the well-protected man, it would be no surprise that his emotional cupboard is so bare, but there still beats a real heart.

Values Under Attack

Now, what I am about to suggest may seem contradictory, but have you ever considered what other reasons there might be for a man to be like a knight in armor? Describing a man as a knight in armor does sound heroic and noble. The world of work is often a competitive, ruthless jungle. Values such as "love your enemies," "pray for those who spitefully use you," "do unto others as you would have them do unto you"—these noble sentiments and virtues sound nice, but they aren't practiced in the real world of work and competition. Perhaps it's more realistic to say "do unto others before they do it unto you." "What is right?" is seldom an ethical question; it usually means "What is the practical way?" You solve a problem, beat the competition—win, survive. A man will use what means he has at his disposal to achieve the right answer, the successful solutions. Proving yourself right becomes more important than what is right. Many men are in conflict with the values they have grown to accept as right and true in the competitive arena of life where they live by another code.

Men often work and compete in an environment where fear is their constant companion and motivator. Life by quota—but when you reach that quota, the next one is always higher. Fear is an older man, who has been productive and faithful to the company, looking over his shoulder at the bright new fair-haired young man bursting with ambition. He is ruthless enough to tell the older man, "I'm here to get your job." There's the fear of being fired, phased out of a job, pressured to quit before your retirement plan goes into effect. This is what a man lives with at work daily.

Trust and love, what are they? To survive, a little paranoia is helpful. Trust too much, or the wrong person, and it will blow up in your face. Love? That feeling doesn't exist in the world ruled by ruthlessness, ambition, jealousy, pettiness, backbiting, and slanderous rumors. Love? Who dares be that foolish and vulnerable? The last man who brought love into the marketplace of life was nailed to a cross. No. The marketplace is not ready for love. Fear and death, that's what life is all about. The emotions that fit are the emotions of cynicism and despair. That's why a man needs a suit of armor. He goes forth each day to slay the dragon or to battle with the black knight. A suit of armor adds to the odds of his returning home nightly, battered but alive. Unfortunately, a man may never take off his suit of armor at home and relax as a human being. In time the suit of armor becomes his skin. He can't remove it.

Contempt for Women?

The next area of exploration in my pilgrimage resulted in my stumbling onto some unexpected findings about myself and other men. It all started with my raising the question to myself about the possibility of deeply programmed contempt for women in me and other men. Do I possess some latent, and maybe some not so latent, hostility toward women? Me? Not me, I tried in vain to reassure myself. If I and other men possess latent hostility toward women, then whence does it stem? Mother? That seemed impossible, because how can a boy resent or dislike, much less be hostile to a "Good Mother"? How can a good boy, like me, resent a "Good Mother" who gives a boy such a great amount of love? I began to play with this thought late one sleepless night. The result—a boy could feel resentment, frustration, hostility from a "Good Mother's" love, when that love is experienced as control and manipulation of a boy's thinking, feelings, and behavior. You feel frustrated and angry, but how do you express those feelings to a "Good Mother"? A "Good Mother's" love can be a millstone around a boy's neck if it creates guilt, dependence, and frustration. After all, mother is always right. How many times does a young man feel the twinge of guilt when mother makes statements like these:

"Look how much I sacrificed for you."

"You don't want to disappoint your mother."

"Now, son, you really don't feel that way."

"Don't worry about how sick I am, go out and have a good time."

You can add your own favorites to this list.

Now if you add the power of a woman's tears to get her way, you can feel very manipulated. Mothers are also so verbally adept that you can be drowned in a sea of words. You give in, not to reason, but to the control of verbosity. Mothers are put on a pedestal, so how can you dare be unhappy when everything is done for your own good? Guilt combined with love is an effective manipulative block that prevents a boy from recognizing his emotions of resentment and antagonism toward his mother.

Now I realize that girls can have it about as hard as boys, but I would like you to consider how much harder it is for a boy to reach manhood when so often the majority of parenting is done by a woman. For a grown man still to be a "mama's boy" is the source for many jokes. It isn't easy for some men to separate themselves from the good, nurturing, loving mother who knows just when to push his guilt buttons and thus keep him emotionally dependent on her and responsible for her happiness. It's much easier for a girl to see what it's like to be a woman, but a boy must somehow be different from his mother and yet not alienate himself from her while he's young or old. Too often a boy's father isn't around enough to help the growth into manhood and provide a male role model.

Robert Johnson in his book *He* states, "No son ever develops into manhood without, in some way, being disloyal to mother. If he remains with his mother, to comfort and console her, then he never gets out of his mother complex."[2]

A son must leave his mother, and this may be seen as betrayal and be very painful to the mother. The son may later return to her, not in a parent-child relationship but as adult to adult. This is more easily achieved when a man has married and formed a new loyalty to his wife. The importance of this truth is stated in the second chapter of *Genesis*, "For this cause shall a man leave father and mother and shall cleave to his wife and they shall become one flesh"(Genesis 2:24).

Feminine Programming

My journey didn't stop there but went deeper into an area which caused a great amount of explorative thinking to new understanding. If a boy is raised primarily by his mother, or even if both parents are active in the upbringing, a boy will receive countless messages of what it's like to be a woman. In the subconscious mind of a man is the programming of a woman. Now be careful, I said the *programming* of a woman, not the urge *to be* a woman. Remember that the subconscious mind is neither good nor bad, and it doesn't recognize the difference between good and bad, fact or fantasy. It's full of power and responds only to what it receives and what's allowed to remain there. The memory banks of the mind receive billions of pictures, words, and messages which are recorded. In a man there are recorded the countless ways a woman feels. Her tenderness, creativity, nurturing, intuition, empathy, passivity, submissiveness, emotionality, and spirituality are recorded in the memory banks of the mind and stored in the subconscious mind.

I wonder if the slightest awareness of the woman in the man by the conscious mind is so threatening and frightening that a man quickly rejects the awareness of the feminine programming in him. Out of fear for his masculinity a man must suppress and retain a tight control over this area of programming in his subconscious mind. This is why a boy is so deeply hurt when he is called a sissy or teased for being a girl.

This has led me to ponder how many young men discover the feminine programming in themselves and jump to the conclusion that they must be homosexuals and not real men after all. I must hasten to add here that I don't want you to think this point I'm discussing is the reason for homosexual behavior. I would be the first to admit that I would be guilty of grossly oversimplifying the etiology of homosexual behavior. I'm wondering though if this might be a factor in developing a self-fulfilling prophecy for homosexuality. For a boy or man too interested in ballet, hair fashion, women's fashion, dancing, and other artistic talents, the admission of interest and talent in areas which have been labeled as feminine might cause a man to conclude, "I must be a homosexual, because that is how I will be labeled if I choose to follow these interests and talents."

Only someone as big as ex–pro football player Roosevelt Grier can do needlepoint in public, and with his size, who would dare call him a queer?

This discovery was new for me, but it had been written about years ago by Carl Jung. Jung had said that each human being is androgynous, with both male and female components in the unconscious. The inner woman in a man Jung calls the "anima" and the inner man in a woman is the "animus."

My pilgrimage has taken me on many unexpected paths and to enlightening discoveries within myself. It now means that I explore the inner woman in me which has been programmed into my subconscious mind. My self-acceptance entails my understanding and awareness of being able to differentiate and live with harmony between the inner woman in me and the outer flesh-and-blood male.

The inner woman in me is simply an acceptance of the reality that I have received a great amount of information about what a woman is. How a woman thinks, reacts, communicates, expresses her emotions, in short, the psychological makeup of a woman is in me. The integration of this information doesn't mean I will begin acting physically like an effeminate man, but that I will be enriched and more complete as a man. I can be more tender and sensitive, aware of all my emotions, not just a few. I will make more sense because what I am feeling on the inside will be readily transparent on the outside. My capacity for empathy, creativity, fantasy, poetry, music, and romance will be enhanced. I will not be ashamed if my dependency needs show. Yes, I will give myself permission to "own" all of me so I can be more alive. I will be me. I will be strong enough to be gentle.

I began to study the history of male-female relations as the result of my discoveries on my pilgrimage. Man's need to dominate woman was an obvious fact. Could it be that a man's need to control a woman is because, deep inside, he's afraid of discovering the inner woman in himself? A woman can make a man feel uneasy, without his knowing why he is uneasy. Women have been treated like objects to be bought and sold—second-class citizens who must be kept in some sort of bondage to a man. This contempt for women is demonstrated, for example, in the ways women are described in derogatory phrases as whores, sluts, dumb broads, tramps, old maids, old bags, little old ladies, and so on.

I have a feeling that some men have discovered the inner woman in themselves and have overreacted to this discovery, so that women have been scapegoated and seen as the sources of evil in the world. The story of Adam and Eve is an ancient story. When God confronted Adam with his disobedience for eating the fruit of the tree of knowledge of good and evil, Adam quickly played the blaming game and accepted no personal responsibility for his "bite" of disobedience. "It was the woman you gave; she gave me the fruit of the tree and I ate." Notice how skillfully Adam is able to blame God for giving him the woman—and "Eve made me do it." Eve was not to be outdone, for she replied, "It was that snake in the grass. He made me do it." Adam was punished, condemned to live by the sweat of his brow, but Eve was severely punished. "I will greatly multiply your pain in childbearing, in pain you shall bring forth children, yet your desire shall be for your husband, and he shall rule over you."

It appears that when people have needed a scapegoat they used either a Jew or a woman. When a man has been threatened by the inner woman in him, out of fear and ignorance he turns to witch-hunts. The reasons for witch-hunts have been many, but still it's hard to believe that men could be so frightened of little old ladies, whose only crime perhaps was being senile, that they burned them as witches. During the Middle Ages, witch-hunts weren't an isolated event here and there that received a lot of publicity. Are you ready for this? At the height of the witch-hunts there were more than four million women burned at the stake.[3] I wonder if this is where Hitler got his idea for exterminating the Jews? A powerful book on the hostility of men toward women is the book on rape, *Against Our Wills*.[4]

This part of my journey has forced me to acknowledge the validity of the women's equal rights movement. It's time we men dealt creatively and honestly with the inner woman in each of us so men won't have to be afraid of losing control of women, and we can stop projecting our fears onto women and blaming them for everything that goes wrong in life. In the same manner it would be healthy for women to acknowledge the inner man in them without resorting to vicious attacks on men, and thus to quit trying to be better men than men. Then a man and a woman could both be self-confident and strong, with an inner harmony and self-acceptance that would permit open and harmonious relationships between them. Both, then, could grow in "personhood" and vitality.

CHECKPOINT

1. When was the last time you cried?

2. When was the last time you felt like crying but didn't?

3. Men are told to bottle up emotions, keep them under control, get a grip on themselves. What are the results of this thinking?

4. What is meant by the phrase "the inner woman in me"? What should you do about the inner woman in you?

—5—

A MAN'S MISTRESS: HIS WORK!

The personal meaning of work will naturally vary from man to man. I was programmed to work hard and enjoy it. I learned to carry the responsibilities of work at an early age. There were lawns to mow, goats to milk, and chickens to feed. At fourteen I was able to join Local 383 of the Laborers Union, because I was the boss's son. Every summer throughout high school I had a job stacking concrete blocks. I was proud I could do a man's work. I saved my money for college. I didn't need a parent to urge me on to go back to school in the fall, because all I had to do was look at my sore, calloused hands, and that was enough for me to know that I wanted to go back to school. My hands were so rough that I couldn't touch a girl for at least a month after I quit for the summer for fear of cutting her skin. Stacking cement blocks in the desert heat was boring work, but I always tried to find some fun with my co-workers. I worked hard and earned their respect, even though I was the boss's son. In fact, if a different shift was short one or two block-stackers, I would be called at home to fill in because I was so lucky to be the boss's son.

Man in a Hurry

I was a young man in a hurry. After my junior year in college, I applied to Northwestern Lutheran Theological Seminary in Minneapolis, Minnesota. I took an overload of course work that spring, went to summer school, and worked nights.

On August 22, Jeannie and I were married. We soon left for Minneapolis.

She was immediately hired as a legal secretary, and I was soon selling Watkins products door-to-door part-time, while going to the seminary full-time. I was a good salesman, not only because I liked people, but because I was becoming a compulsive work addict. Freezing weather and snow storms didn't stop me. If I got too cold I would take a swallow of Watkins liniment and that would provide a warm glow.

That summer we returned to Phoenix so I could attend summer school for my college education.

When we returned to Minneapolis for my second year of seminary, I was surprised to be asked to serve as an interim pastor for the church at which I had done some youth work during my first year in seminary. I was shocked and pleased to be asked to help as a pastor. Here I was, just twenty-two, one year of seminary, and I was to work in a church of about one thousand adults.

Two of the seminary professors who belonged to the church would help do the baptisms, marriages, and communion services and help me with the preaching. It was not a very spiritual meeting with the church council that Sunday when I was asked how much money it would take for me to quit my Watkins job and accept the position as an interim pastor. I told them how much money I was earning and I was hired. Now I felt an added responsibility on my shoulders. I was determined to prove myself in this church and still attend classes as a full-time seminary student. The work in the parish took every spare minute; no, I *gave* the parish every spare moment. As you can imagine, this meant I spent more and more time away from Jeannie and our one-year-old son, Mike. It was a major concession on my part to watch Mike when Jeannie went to that cold, damp basement to do the washing. She promised to hurry so I could go back to work. To provide her with company while I was gone, either at school or working at the church, I bought her a television set to serve as my replacement. Since none of the married seminarians in our apartments owned a television set in 1952, Jeannie had lots of company. Wasn't that thoughtful of me? The ironic and sad part of it was that I did not see anything wrong in what I was doing. After all, I had to support a family and attend seminary.

Working at St. Mark's Lutheran Church provided me with an income and a unique opportunity to gain invaluable experience. It was also spiritual work, so that made it even more valid. For two years, seven days a week, starting at 8:00 A.M. and finishing my day around 10:30 P.M. became a normal routine. A dangerous behavioral pattern was developed.

Since I was a young man in a hurry, I graduated from college in 1953 with high distinction. I graduated from three years of seminary in 1954 with the added plus of two years of practical pastoral experience thrown in for good measure. I was all of twenty-three years of age when I was ordained. My motor was racing because I was accustomed to working at high speeds. I had become a workaholic.

I was sent to Canoga Park, California, to develop a home-mission congregation. I was very grateful for my training as a door-to-door salesman for Watkins, because that's all I did for months—rang doorbells! In the wave of new subdivisions being built, I was a door-to-door salesman for religion. One day as I was approaching a home, a man of the house shouted, "Stop, we already have two of whatever you are selling."

I replied, "I doubt that, sir."

"Well," he responded, "are you selling insurance?"

"I agree that in a way I am an insurance man."

"Well, what company do you represent?" he asked.

"Celestial and Fire," I replied.

He mumbled the name to himself several times and said, "Never heard of it. Are you sure you are an insurance man?"

Then I told him who I was, and it hit him what I had said about "Celestial and Fire." He roared with laughter.

I lived my life by the numbers. I set a goal of ringing one hundred doorbells per month for the first three months. Finally we held our first service in a women's clubhouse that we had rented.

Jeannie's mom was with us for a visit, and the night before the first service, she voiced her greatest fear: "What if no one comes to the services tomorrow?"

Our first service was a success numberwise and religionwise. Numbers for me became the way I measured my success; I wasn't alone. Every time a group of ministers would gather together it was all number talk. How many people were attending church? How many members have joined your church lately? When do you break ground on your new building, or how is the new building progressing and how much did it cost? The more numerical success I experienced the harder I worked. I was at the right place at the right time. It was no wonder that our church, the Lutheran Church of the Resurrection, when it was officially organized the following spring, set a record for the United Lutheran Church of America.

Did I relax and enjoy my achievement? Not on your life. The next month we plunged into a building-fund drive. I was an ambitious young pastor with a great amount of get-up-and-go. I rationalized my responsibilities as a husband and father.

I was home by five o'clock every day, and I did take Monday off. I helped with dinner, played with Mike, bathed him, and put him to bed.

I was also out of the house by seven every evening making more calls or attending meetings. And by ten-thirty or eleven I was home for the night. I was always willing to make just one more call. I was so wound up it seemed natural. I didn't know how to slow down or to say no to people and not feel guilty. I had the credentials for an energetic, successful, dynamic young pastor.

Jeannie would have described me in different terms. That's the trouble with wives, they just don't understand us hardworking men. We work so hard for the family. A man has to provide for his family. My wife had the ridiculous idea that a man should provide for the emotional needs of his wife and children as well. She had the strange idea that a paycheck isn't enough and that my work was an ego trip. Jeannie kept trying to talk to me about companionship and communication, talking about something other than my work. She wanted me to make time for her when she wasn't at the end of the line. I guess she hadn't believed me when I informed her before we were married that she came third in my life. First, God; second, other people; and third, Jeannie. Then, painfully, she believed.

Now, as I write about this crazy man I have an uneasy, nauseous feeling in my stomach. I think I am going to be sick.

Changing Gears

One of the advantages of the ministry was the annual month's vacation. I surprised myself with the ease with which I could relax, forget about work, and rediscover my wife and our children. Maybe this one month a year was a lifesaver. I knew vaguely that something was wrong with my life, and I discovered that more and more I looked forward to the next year's vacation. It became very obvious to me that just when I returned from one vacation, I would catch myself counting the months till next year's vacation. I was shocked to realize that I was living for one month a year, while the intervening months were just a blur of frantic activity. When you live only one month a year, the years of your life go by very fast.

In previous chapters I talked about my compulsive drive for approval, and how I finally accepted and approved of myself. This helped me look within and make decisions to change my life's addictive pattern. I began to change and stop my rush to die. Taking the cure for work addiction is like all other addictive behavior in that it's hard to change and easy to slip back into the addictive behavioral patterns.

A man's work is his life, and for some of us that's all there is to our lives. It's easy to get out of balance and become a one-dimensional man. Jeannie's greatest rival has always been my preoccupation with my career and my books. I wish I could state it differently, but at that time I was so self-centered. As I write this I want to deny it, but I was so wrapped up in my own important world that all I had on my mind, most of the time, was myself and my work. I still have a long way to go in that area. I wonder how many women have married their man because he's ambitious and a hard worker who will always provide the security and necessities of life—only to have the rude awakening that what they have is an ambitious hardworking workaholic.

At thirty-two I was seeking a change of pace. I took some time to look at myself and grow, and decided to apply at several graduate schools to earn a doctoral degree in psychology.

I wasn't accepted then. One school said I was too old and probably too set in my mind to learn anything new. They also felt I might be too rigid because I was a minister. I accepted a call to Grace Lutheran Church in Richmond, California. I was able to shift down some. I was still in conflict between wanting to be a psychologist and remaining in the parish ministry. My blood pressure began to climb, and the physician warned me that if I didn't slow down, I could have a coronary in ten years. So again I decided to apply for graduate school. I was finally accepted into a graduate department in psychology. I worked hard and fast to get through school before the money ran out I went to school year-round and spent two years as an intern psychologist at the state hospital part-time. I completed a four-year program in two years, but I deluded myself into believing I wasn't falling back into my workaholic life-style. I thought I was learning to say no and not feel guilty, but I was only kidding myself.

When the drug epidemic exploded in our state in 1968, I found myself giving seventy to eighty speeches a year and trying to be a modern-day Paul Revere, charging around the state warning the people of the dangers of drugs and how they were destroying our children. I was on another crusade. I had fallen back into my workaholic ways.

Days became a blur and on Friday nights I would collapse in exhaustion. Sometimes I would say, "Jeannie, just let me lie on the floor and relax a moment and watch TV." Soon I'd be sound asleep.

My life became those children's faces, looks of anguished parents, names of strange drugs from orange sunshine to STP to junk—and endless speeches, pressures, and fatigue. In February of 1971 a federal grant arrived to help finance our drug program, and I decided to go back to private practice, but that's another story.

I am finding more balance to my life, and I think maybe I'm cured, or at least have arrested my workaholic behavior. I don't live life by the numbers anymore. I no longer need a crusade.

Karl Menninger once described adolescence as that period in a person's life which begins at puberty and ends with the acquisition of wisdom. Maybe I've acquired some wisdom at last.

The Overrating of Success

I believe we've highly overrated the life of the professional man. The more education a man receives, ironically, the more hours he works. Business executives are in the same jet stream of investing so much of their life energy in their world of the business-and-success syndrome. Executive wives, like the wives of innumerable professional men, are often puzzled and bewildered by a man's devotion to his business. It isn't uncommon for an executive's wife to blame and resent the corporation for its exacting demands on her husband's loyalty and time. Much unhappiness is bred by having to move from home to home, continually unsettled, with the children changing schools, just so a man can move up in the corporate structure. The man knows that to turn down a move and promotion is to face the fear of never being offered another promotion. To blame and criticize the husband's corporation is to fail to recognize that it is his life, his ego, his career, and his choices that a wife is criticizing. He's not the victim of a corporation, he's a part of the corporation.

There's a new trend in industry to realize and recognize that a man's worth to a company is enhanced by the harmony of his home life. Seminars are being conducted for the executive wife, and they're finally seeking to work out some of these destructive patterns that destroy the family life of executives.

In 1974 Dr. Robert J. Samp conducted a survey of 1700 people over the age of 80, including 129 who were 100 years old or older. He said, "We didn't find any intense, driving, highly competitive business-executive types in the whole bunch."

He reported believing that today's uptight life-style is a major factor in killing men before their time. Dr. Samp suggests that the key to living a longer, healthier, and happier life lies in identifying the primary stress factors in life, and changing.[1] These stress factors are related to how a person is programmed, his life-style, his diet, his exercise or lack of exercise, and his attitudes toward work, life, and death.

Often a man's self-worth is interwoven with how he earns a living. You ask a man, "Who are you?" He will likely reply by telling you his occupation. If this livelihood is closely tied to the ups and downs of the economy, he's very vulnerable in times of economic lows and unemployment. The recession of the 1970s was characterized by the unemployment of high-level executives. The hundred-thousand-dollar man was fired because he was too expensive in hard times. Stock-market executives pounded the street looking for any job. There were countless executives who, after they lost their jobs, could not face telling their wives or children. They left home each morning, briefcase in hand, as if nothing had happened, and then frantically spent the day searching for a position in a job market that was flooded with similar individuals. They arrived home at the normal hour. The hope was to find employment before savings were spent. Only at the last moment would they break the devastating news to the wife and children. They would be forced to sell their beautiful home, the yacht, give up the country-club membership, because there was no job, nor any prospect of a new one. A man at this point is extremely vulnerable and close to committing suicide, because his self-worth is so closely identified with his career's success or failure.

The Mirage of Security

In life's search it's hard to accept that security is an illusive mirage because we live in such a fast-changing and ever more complex world.

Milton Mayeroff believes that "basic certainty requires outgrowing the need to feel certain, to have absolute guarantees as to what is or what will be. Instead, if we think of basic certainty as including deep-seeded security, it also includes being vulnerable and giving up the one occupation of trying to be secure."[2]

I've always considered myself a high-risk person. I'm not afraid to go out on a limb and try something new. My sense of security comes from within myself as a result of a deep-seated image I have of myself. I'm not afraid to start again in my life and experience new careers and opportunities.

Judith M. Bardwick in her study *Men and Work* said that the most outstanding characteristic of highly successful men was that they were not only high-risk people, they were also risk creators. Men such as these seem willing to throw security, and all the safety and comfort it implies, into the air, gambling on the possibility that they, and the world they have juggled, will land upright. These men create risk and keep their lives in constant flux. Never sedentary, never secure, no matter how safe they have felt, or how convenient or calm were their surroundings, they were usually willing to throw themselves headlong into new areas. Success was seldom guaranteed. Their confidence came not from their savings accounts or possessions, but because they believed within that they had the qualities to build meaningful relationships in any sphere.[3]

I don't propose that because I have made many changes in my career and risked starting over anew, every man should do the same—far from it. Each man must plumb his own self to discover what is his secret source of security. His security needn't be in things, or even in his work, but in his confidence, in his ability to change and to grow.

Meaningful Work

The meaning of work varies for each man. I admit that I've been talking about the category of men whose work is their life and is the end in itself. For the large majority of men, work is a means to an end, such as supporting a family, buying a home, a car, a television set, and so on. It serves to make their life away from their work more enjoyable.

One doesn't have to be a great, perceptive social scientist to be aware that for many men their jobs are dull, drab, monotonous, and boring. The blue-collar blues are for real. Their heart isn't in their work even though their pay may be very good. The ethic of work for the sake of working is not turning them on. Assembly-line work that demands little challenge or responsibility leads to low job satisfaction and a high level of anxiety. The loss of pride through repetitive work results in absenteeism, tardiness, high job turnover, apathy, or even industrial sabotage and theft. A man who doesn't care about his work is also destroying his own self-worth. He needs to find meaning, validation, and growth outside his work as a person. I've heard that today it's too easy to reward a man for not working steadily because of high unemployment benefits, union benefits, and food stamps. I wonder what percentage of the unemployed are those who have discovered that it's just as financially rewarding to work spasmodically and then live off "the benefits" for not working?

A man who trades his personal pride and responsibility for the easy route of being supported by someone else is slowly eroding away his own identity and self-worth. Taking away, or giving away, a man's pride in himself can result in a frustrated, potentially violent man.

While a man's work is an important expression of himself, I hope I haven't overemphasized the negative aspects. The genius of a man is revealed in his dreams, his dedication, and what he creates. When I study the lives of great men in history, I am awed by their spirit, determination, courage, and talent. Theirs is more than just an ego trip. Man is created in the image of God; to be creative is a part of his essence. To have a dream, to answer a challenge, to solve problems are parts of man's greatness. We should not lose sight of this.

CHECKPOINT

1. In ten words or less, what does work mean to you?

2. As you think about priorities in your life, where does your work fit? Has it always been that way?

3. When someone asks, "Who are you?" how do you respond?

4. Dr. Robert Samp reported that the key to living a longer, healthier, and happier life lies in identifying the primary stress factors in life, and changing. Seven of those stress factors are listed in this chapter. What are they?

5. What is the basis of your security in life? Do you agree that "Security is an illusive mirage"?

6. Are you a high-risk person? Judith Bardwick says that the most outstanding characteristic of highly successful men is that they are not only high-risk people, but also risk creators. Who in the Bible were high-risk people and also risk creators?

VULNERABILITY

part three

—6—

THE VULNERABILITY OF SUCCESS AND FAILURE

One of the most frightening aspects of my pilgrimage has been the awareness of my own self-destructive behavior.

I've realized that at times I've been self-destructive, but I've adroitly pushed it back into my subconscious mind. My self-destructive behavior doesn't mean that I have contemplated committing suicide as a serious option to life. In my case, I have noticed a destructive pattern when I am successful. I began to look at my own behavior and that of other men who demonstrate their self-destructive behavior at the zenith of their success.

It seems paradoxical that success is such a sought-after goal. Why does an important value trigger self-destructive behavior in some men? For example, take former President Nixon. He had been defeated many times in his political career and counted out by others, and even by himself, but his consuming desire to achieve success finally resulted in an overwhelming victory at the polls. The outsider from Whittier, California, had finally made it to the top of the world. Success was his. Nixon had a passion for his place in history. Then came his Watergate, and the most destructive decision of all, to keep the tapes when he could have destroyed them. His knowledge as a lawyer, politician, and rational human being failed him. He set himself up for his own self-destruction at the time of his greatest achievement and acclaim.

Self-Destructive Behavior

Where does this inner self-destructive behavior begin? Is it born out of the feelings arising from low self-esteem that generate an enormous psychic energy and drive a person to prove himself to be something special to others?

"I'll show them someday. I made it to the top and they were wrong about me. When I'm at the top, they'll all have to look up to me then and eat crow."

If you make it to the top then you are a success. You've proven to everyone who thought you couldn't make it that you could make it. Maybe the only one whom you haven't convinced is yourself. Even at the pinnacle of success there is a haunting feeling. What are you doing up here? Will you be able to stay at this place of success?

I will never forget the strange uneasy feelings I experienced after we moved into our beautiful home in the desert in Paradise Valley, Arizona. I never dreamed that we would own such a home, with such a magnificent view—a home that was more valuable than the one that my parents lived in. Of course dreams do come true, but I had fleeting thoughts of, "What right do I have to deserve a home like this?" I had a distinct feeling that if I wasn't careful I could make one or two bad judgments in my life and lose that home and all that was important.

It seems there are only two ways to go when you have

reached a level of success. One is more success. The other is failure.

Years ago there was a story of ten millionaires who achieved financial success as young men. A few years later only one of them still had his money and success.

Is there a danger for finding success or reaching it too soon or too young?

Professional athletes have this particular problem. They make it to the top, are successful, personally and financially, at a very young age, and then in a few years it's all over. The step down, from the heights of the world of professional athletes with its status and financial rewards, is a long one, and the impact is the jolt of reality that it's over. What do I do now? How can I ever earn that much money again? You were king for a day, but now night has fallen. The adjustment isn't an easy one. The high living, the spotlight—they've a nice place in the sun, and it's often a tragedy when night falls.

Fear of Failure

I wonder if the fear of failure and of losing everything gained is a reason for some of the queasy feeling inside us when we reach success? Are we afraid of failure? There are no courses on how to be a successful failure. A man is never so vulnerable, in such confused pain, as when he has failed.

Now this isn't true of all men. I will never forget a business card I was given when I was fifteen years old. On the card it said, "World's Most Successful Failure." Here was a happy man, whose eyes had the look of a pixie, and he was always beginning to tell a story, a joke, or to make you the butt of the joke.

He had developed a hobby. For Christmas he would think of an unusual gift to give prominent people. For example, what would surprise and please Winston Churchill, Franklin Roosevelt, and people of that stature? Jerry would think of an unusual gift and send it. It worked. He received personal letters from leaders all over the world.

Jerry made an impression on me with his attitude toward life, from the good times to the ones we don't speak of, the times of failure. He had no fear of failure, and so when he failed, he would say, "What could you expect from the world's most successful failure?" and he would try again.

The fear of making a mistake is the monkey that is placed on so many of our backs. "What will the neighbors think?" "Don't do anything to disgrace your father." "Wait till your father gets home and hears what you've done." Boy, you just couldn't wait to see dad that night. The tension of waiting to be punished for making a mistake was the worst part of all.

In professional fields we know that the greatest fear of the physician is the death of a patient. This is that black specter that haunts their professional life. Ironically, the physician does all that he can medically do, and the patient dies. He did not fail. The physician isn't God, and he should not assume personal responsibility for the patient's dying. The patient died because, as a human, a physician can do only so much, and that's all. Death will win, and we will all die. For death is a fact of life.

The fear of failure is noticed with dentists. Their greatest fear is that of failure and rejection by a patient. If a patient has lost a filling, he will sometimes say, "I had this done eight years ago, why did it fall apart?" Or, "This porcelain crown broke." They may not tell the dentist that they were chewing on ice cubes at the time. The dentist will internalize this as blame. He will condemn himself as a failure.

Losing and failing are almost anti-American. A football coach can have a winning record year after year, and even—a rarity of a lifetime—an undefeated season, but woe be to the coach and his staff and players if, after a perfect season, next year's team has a losing season. The fans boo and spill booze on the coach as he walks out of the stadium. The alumni are up in arms, "What will this losing season do for our plans for expanding the stadium? What about the money for the new clubhouse? It's suddenly drying up." The fear of continuing failure produces a demon of fear that soon traps coaches, players, and fans, and they forget all the years of winning seasons. Even the memory of the perfect season, the post-season bowl triumph, has now left a sour taste, because what can you do for an encore to a perfect undefeated season and a high national ranking? Get a new coach! A winner.

Richard Halverson wrote these words, "Somebody has to lose! The trouble is in our culture. Everybody is conditioned to win, so losing is often traumatic, for the loser—for his friends—for his family, because we have made the winner our status symbol. We don't know how to lose. We are so success oriented we find it almost impossible to accept failure. Nobody cares for a 'loser'. Success is god. Despite which, failing may be one of the most reliable character builders. Losing may deepen understanding, appreciation for others, sympathy, ability to identify with the needy and produce authentic humility. Winning can harden character, result in arrogance, impatience with others, contempt for less fortunate. Losing can soften character. Winning can inflate ego . . . losing mature it. Not that winning is wrong, but somebody has to lose, and it is important to recognize this fact, accept it as a reality in life, prepare for it and learn from it."[1]

Fear of failure makes little people who are so afraid that a mistake will trip them up and destroy them. They become tense and uptight and accident-prone.

Years ago I heard of a group of statisticians in New York who had some time on their hands, and one of the group suggested, "Just for the fun of it, let's study broken bones in people." Everyone breaks a bone. That was the assumption. They collected their data and it revealed an unexpected finding. A person's religion was a significant factor in who had broken bones. People who belonged to an authoritarian religion with a strong emphasis on fear, whether it be as an Orthodox Jew, a Roman Catholic, or a fundamental Protestant, had the highest frequency of broken bones. Members of less authoritarian religions, which do not emphasize fear, had fewer broken bones. For example, a person who had an authoritarian religion could be crossing the street and see the light turn yellow; instead of racing across the street, he might impulsively turn back to the corner to avoid breaking the law in crossing the street on a red light. But the impulsive dash back to the curb could cause him to be hit by a car turning the corner, for the driver had not expected a person to retreat impulsively to the street corner.

I remember a friend of mine whose father growled like a tough general. This father didn't spank his children, but he had such an authoritarian voice he did instill fear. One afternoon my friend was driving a pickup truck along the edge of a field, and the front end of the truck suddenly went down into a small ditch that had been dug to drain the water from the field. He panicked for fear of what his father would do if he discovered that he had the truck stuck in the ditch. So he raced across the field, jumped into a jeep, and sped to the pickup truck. He tied a chain to the rear axle of the truck, jumped into the jeep, put it in reverse, shot backward, and snapped the front axle of the jeep. Now he was in real trouble. If he had just used a shovel to make a slant in the ditch he could have backed the truck out, but his fear of his father threw off his thinking ability. As a result, he acted impulsively and with disastrous effects.

Hugh Prather wrote these words, "Perfectionism is slow death. If everything were to turn out just like I would want it to, then I would never experience anything new; my life would be an endless repetition of stale success. When I make a mistake I experience something unexpected. I sometimes react to making a mistake as if I had betrayed myself. My fear of making a mistake seems to be based on the hidden assumption that I am potentially perfect, and that if I can just be very careful, I will not fall from Heaven, but a mistake is a declaration of the way I am. A jolt to the way I intend. A reminder I am not dealing with the facts. When I have listened to my mistakes, I have grown."[2]

When I have listened to my own mistakes, I have grown, even though the growth has been painful and some of my favorite illusions about myself have been shattered. I realize that I often make the most progress on my knees. As a psychotherapist I have had to stand guard over my need to rescue people who actually didn't want to be rescued; and if they did, they would rather do it themselves. I did learn a high tolerance for failure as a therapist. I realize that people have a right to their own lives and the right to their destruction. All I have to ask of myself is to be there and try one more time, but I try not to call myself a failure.

Setting Ourselves Up for Failure

I'd like to tell you the story of how I became the president of a cloud. It all has to do with success and how I set myself up for failure. As I look back now, I realize that I've had a difficult time with my hat size when I've been in the spotlight too long and have been looked up to as an exceptional person. My ego needs have become my blinders. I would see only what I wanted, and ignore what I needed to see. I would lose my ability to listen to people and wouldn't heed the warnings that I was beginning to get into trouble. I changed. I began to believe my own fantastic propaganda.

In scuba diving we talk about the danger of the rapture of the deep, of how a person, once there's too much nitrogen in his system, begins to act crazy. I sometimes feel that there is a rapture of success that also produces its own kind of craziness. It happens when a person begins to believe so much in his invincibility and grandiosity that no one can touch him. I began to believe some of this nonsense. I changed. I was a success, but I didn't continue to use the qualities that brought me to success. I became the president of a cloud. I knew I was lonely being the president of a cloud, but when I came back to earth it was a jarring jolt.

Here's how my cloud illusion grew, and fell. During the drug crisis in Phoenix I became so involved in trying to rescue young people and set up treatment programs, that I turned my private practice into a nonprofit foundation. I worked day and night. I had $2500 in the bank and I hired nine people to become staff members. I was on television and radio. It didn't take much in those days to become an expert on drug abuse, but I became an instant expert. I was a success, and the more I worked, and the harder I tried to maintain that success, the more grandiose I became, the more I began to lose touch with people and with my own sense of reality.

To be honest, my feet were pretty far off the ground. I knew something was going wrong, and I couldn't stop it. I heard there was a plot afoot to have me fired. But nobody could touch me, I was above being fired. After all, I was the president of my own foundation. Yet the day before the federal money came to Phoenix to help pay for the salaries for all the different treatment centers and education programs, I was fired from my own foundation. I was told I was no longer needed.

This was a devastating experience for me, though I knew it was coming. I went home and cried, my wife cried, and the kids cried.

My twelve-year-old daughter, Jan, said, "Daddy, tonight you're supposed to go out to Parents Anonymous (a self-help group for parents of drug abusers) to give a speech. How do you feel about going out tonight and talking?"

I said, "Jan, I hurt too much to go out and face the public tonight."

She said to me, "Dad, let's think about it for a while." Later in the afternoon she said to me, "Daddy, I think you need to go to the meeting tonight and give yourself away one more time. I'll be awake when you get home, and you can tell me how it went."

I said, "You're right."

I went to that meeting, and I talked about all the things that I needed to hear—about how not to live with bitterness, hate, resentment, and how to get back up off the floor once you have been knocked down. Keep on living, and keep on loving.

Only one man in the audience knew what had happened to me that day, for in the previous week he had been fired from the crisis center. After the meeting, he came up to me and said, "Ken, how could you go and talk the way you did tonight after what you went through this morning?"

I said, "When you listen to the children you are in good hands."

It's been hard for me to look at that experience. I know that there are other times that I have been fired, and I didn't realize that I'd been a party to setting myself up, that I was not just an innocent victim. Out of these painful experiences I've made the vital decisions not to live with self-pity, because I will not allow someone else to push the buttons of my negative tapes.

It took me years to admit how I became self-destructive and set myself up for my own fall from being the president of a cloud. I bought an old print of a painting of a cowboy sleeping on a cloud and daydreaming to remind me of my destructiveness and my failures, so I could continue to learn from my mistakes.

I've also developed a philosophy of life. When I've been fired, I refuse to work for a place that will not hire me. After all, a person has to have some principles in life.

I have also developed another simple beatitude of life that goes like this: "Blessed is he who, when he falls, still remembers how to bounce like a ball."

Learning From Mistakes

I've had years to listen and learn from my mistakes. This has also given me perspective to observe and listen to other men as they strive for success. So much of a man's energy is directed toward his goal of success, that as long as he's struggling to reach the goal, he's not self-destructive. The problem of destructive behavior occurs when he reaches his goal.

One of the mistakes that I have noticed men will make is that they don't set new goals for themselves once they achieve success. For example, many medical and dental students are married, and their wives work to support them through their graduate education. Their goal is to complete this education. They both sacrifice. The wife sacrifices to help the husband get through, and she doesn't complain too much because she shares her husband's goal to finish. The couple may have little time together, and less money, so they put off time for enjoyment until they are through graduate school and finally set up in their own practice.

Some very sad and distressing things begin to happen after the completion of graduate school. Many of the husbands divorce their wives, and seek a woman who will now fit into their life as a successful professional man's wife. The original couple's goal was to finish school. These goals provided them with the energy to reach that goal, but they failed to reset their goals for their marriage as a successful professional couple. These dumped wives are not too thrilled with the reality that they were used by their husbands.

This characteristic of using people to reach one's goal is all too common, but it can become the seed of a man's self-destruction. A man becomes caught up with blind ambition, and he begins to spend more and more time and energy. One success isn't enough. Earning so much money is never enough. There has to be more. He is caught in the greed machine with longer hours of work consuming his career. He begins to develop into a lopsided man. He can provide financial security for his wife and children, new homes and new cars, swimming pool, memberships in country clubs, but there is little left of him to invest in the marriage and his children. I sometimes feel that behind every successful married man is a very lonely woman.

When I recall the years that I was so busy with my occupation, and how lonely Jeannie was, it seems a miracle that she's still with me. She's shown an awful lot of patience and love, and I realize that in my drive to success, I could have sacrificed that which was most important to me, my wife and my home. For what does it profit a man if he gains a whole world, but loses the purpose of his life, as well as the people who make it purposeful?

The Rapture of Success

This "rapture of success" is a psychological phenomenon that I have noticed within myself and other men. It's as if we are always waiting to test and challenge our success. Sometimes we will take business risks we know are shaky, but we will still risk it all. It's as if we have reached a point of being superman, or maybe it goes back to that insecurity of trying to prove ourself one more time. I haven't thought of this before, but when I was a young boy in Houston, Texas, my friends and I used to climb up and down train trestles. Sometimes one would get on one track and the other on another track, and then we would race barefooted across the bayou on this train trestle. When a train would come, we would climb over the sides of the trestle and hang on the sides as the train shook us with its vibrations. I remember walking across the boards, the support columns between pylons of the trestle, knowing there was a flooded bayou below us. Was this just childish exploration, devil-may-care play, or was it a part of that intrinsic fear of always having to prove and challenge even death?

This "rapture of success"—I wonder if this is one of the reasons why so many physicians and dentists make such dangerous pilots. They begin to believe in their "Dr. God" egos, their invincibility and their grandiosity, to a point that even weather reports pertain to other pilots, not themselves. In reality they are very high-risk pilots to fly with.

It seems also that success creates an illusion and delusion of grandeur that makes you an instant expert in many fields. This makes you a prime target for people who come along with a get-rich-quick scheme. You forget that the person who had the get-rich-quick scheme doesn't mean that you are going to get rich quick, but that he is. Is there a guilt that goes with having money and success? Do we feel obligated to spend until we've brought ourselves down into debt again so that we feel comfortable?

What is success? Have we ever really stopped to have a course in how to become a successful person and stay successful? It would be interesting to have a discussion on just what is a successful man. Success according to whom, and by what standards? Success too often has been measured in terms of quantity and not quality of life.

> *I have a rendezvous with success.*
> *I rush and frantically push my body to extreme distress.*
> *These words echo in my mind—compete, compete, and never*
>   *retreat.*
> *Strive for the best, so fast my heart does beat.*
> *Be perfect, no less. Then one day I will have success.*
> *But lost in the din is the voice within crying.*

Stop! Be wise. Is this the life you prize?
A collection of things gathered while rushing to die but never
finding out the 'why'![3]

CHECKPOINT

1. What is meant by self-destructive behavior? Can you give an example of it in your own life?

2. Why is it natural to fear failure?

3. Give an example of a Bible character who was afraid to fail.

4. How do you cope with the experience of failing?

5. What was your latest success? By what criteria do you call it a success?

—7—
THE CRISIS OF THE MIDDLE-AGED MAN

"For the wise and fool both die, and in the days to come both will be long forgotten. So now I hate life because it is all so irrational, all is foolishness, chasing the wind" (Ecclesiastes 2:16, 17).

A middle-aged man can experience some strange and dangerous times for himself. It is a time of high risk for marriages. The fastest growing divorce rate is for marriages of twenty to thirty years.

It can be a time of depression for a man, even without any outer precipitating factors. There often is a self-destructiveness that bewilders wife, friends, and business associates. A man who has driven himself to reach a goal in life, or make his business a success, suddenly doesn't care if his business fails or not. It is as though he has reached his peak of success and only hears Peggy Lee singing, "Is That All There Is?"

By definition, middle age is the span of years from thirty-five to fifty-five. I used to deny being middle-aged by kidding myself that I will be middle-aged next year. Then when I turned fifty-six, I felt I would love to be middle-aged again. Maybe I'll extend the upper limits of middle age to seventy-five.

Where Is Our Support System?

You hear a lot about the crisis of the middle-aged man these days, but where is the help? Who can a middle-aged man go to for medical and psychological assistance and support? Women have their "ob-gyn" physicians to go to for information, physicals, hormone pills or shots, and to be told what to expect emotionally as well as physically. A woman during these years has an elaborate support system, with friends to talk with, as well as her physician.

But where does a middle-aged man go for support? What can be done for him? A man has never been given permission to talk about his emotions, fears, and doubts.

One man expressed this frustration to me with these words, "I don't know how to explain to someone the inner rage I feel deep inside. I am fearful that anyone I would express these feelings to would think I was ready to flip out. I don't even know what this inner rage is all about. I do know that my wife is puzzled and scared because of the rage she feels when I lash out at her for no reason. Am I angry at the realization that I'm getting older? Or feeling depressed because some of my cherished dreams of youth have never come true for me? Is part of my rage because of the realization that so much of my life is gone, man, really gone, and how little I have lived? There is a rage burning inside. I feel like hitting someone or something. Maybe I am really mad at myself, whoever that is!"

The Chinese word for crisis is written by combining the symbols for the words *danger* and *opportunity*. The middle years are just that for a man . . . a time of danger, and a time for opportunity.

Problems of Adjustment

I became aware of the danger of the middle years when I was in my late twenties. A friend of mine, in his forties, committed suicide. What puzzled me so was, here was an outwardly happy man with a good marriage, and as far as I could discern, no precipitating factors or changes in life that would cause him to end his life. He was very active in church and a joy to know. The puzzle was never solved as to why one Sunday morning he shot himself.

I began to read about suicide and the danger of a man's middle years. One thing became apparent. We didn't know very much about the middle-aged man and the psychological crisis he faces. One significant factor is his vocational life. Say, for example, a man has always been self-employed, or has worked in a family grocery store and is people-oriented. When the family grocery store is bought out by a large food chain, he can't adjust to the impersonal structure of a large supermarket, so he quits. Since he has done little else but this type of work and is middle-aged, he has a difficult time in finding new employment. Finally he becomes a night janitor at a community college. Now here is a man, who loves working with people, suddenly working a solitary job as a night janitor. Reason enough to commit suicide? I don't know, but reason enough for me to realize that the male climactic years have too long been ignored, much less understood.

Since we have become such a youth-oriented society, there comes an anxiety in some women and some men after they turn thirty. Women look in mirrors to check for "crow's feet" around the eyes, drooping eyelids, brown spots in the skin from the liver, gray hair, and fatty deposits on the body. When a man looks in the mirror, he sees a Greek god—until one day when he is middle-aged he looks in the mirror and doesn't see a Greek god. He is shocked and says, "Oh, God, is that really me with the thinning hair, jowly cheeks, bags under the eyes, a shrunken chest, suffering from 'lap-belta,' the stomach lapping over the belt?"

But, alas, he realizes that the mirror on the wall is not lying. He had always thought of himself as a "macho man;" now he is a middle-aged man with too "mucha" in the wrong places.

After a period of mild depression, such a man begins to try to recapture his youth. He plans to go on a diet, start exercising, maybe jog a couple of miles each morning.

The next morning he starts to jog around the block, but halfway around the block he is coughing, breathing hard, and his heart sounds like a bongo drum. He sits down on the curb, hanging his head between his knees, when a fellow jogger, naturally young and physically trim, stops to ask if he is all right. After reassuring the jogger that he is fine, it hits him. He thinks, "I was about to die! Wow!" He decides that he had better watch it or he might check out early in life like his friend, Sam, did when he was jogging around the block.

His goal of being a "macho" man is shattered. He had been programmed to believe that he must always be a tower of strength and never reveal any weakness or fear, but now he realizes this is no longer possible.

Each man will experience this period in his life in different ways. I realized that even my knowledge of the symptoms of middle age and my being a psychologist didn't mean I was immune to the problems of this period of my life. My first reaction was one of denial—"I'm not middle-aged"—as if it was something awful.

To be truthful, the forties were my favorite years, especially the forties that are closer to thirty than the forties that are closer to fifty. It's true for me that this period of my life changed me from being such an outwardly directed doer, to a more introspective, pensive person. The fact that I'm writing this book is a point that speaks for itself. I couldn't have written this book earlier in my life, nor would I have felt the need to embark on this pilgrimage.

Middle age is obviously the midpoint in life. At forty-five I made the decision to live to ninety. When I was a child I couldn't wait to grow up, but this business of growing up isn't a matter of declaring that you are, at twenty-one, a man. Life is a series of cycles and changes, and with each cycle there are new changes, new challenges, and new crises. The crisis of the newly married, the crisis of the first child, the first teenager, the first disappointment in relationships, the struggle to earn a living, and maintain the standard of living to which you've become accustomed. Marriage is hard work, so you have the crisis of the seven-year itch, which is a critical time.

Man puts so much of his life and energy into his work, but the road to the top is not a steady upward climb. There's often a series of failures, set backs, regroupings, or changes of jobs. Sometimes a man reaches a point of despair. Middle age can be a period of time when you realize that what you're doing is what you have to do, and you're not very good at it.

The middle years can then become a time of special crisis and danger. Men are warned to be understanding of wives when they enter the menopause, but who warns a man, or his wife, of what to expect of the middle years for a man?

The Collision of Youthful Dreams and Reality

For some men it's the time when the jolting reality of death and the death of youthful dreams collide. This shakes any man to the core. He looks back and sees all the years of struggle to reach the top and realizes maybe there are no new surprises for him in life.

If he loses a job now, he discovers that potential employers consider him too old, even though he futilely protests, "I'm not a young man leapfrogging from one job to another. I'll be steady. I'll be a reliable worker. What do you mean I'm too old?"

"Sorry, sir, company policy. You see, we just don't hire anyone over forty-three years of age."

Or, he may be told that it isn't that he's too old, but that he's overqualified for the job, and therefore, wouldn't be happy with the opening. The man pleads, "I want the job; I need the job. Look, I won't be unhappy with less responsibility. I would like less responsibility."

"But we don't want you to be unhappy with our firm. Good day, sir."

As he walks away, his shoulders slump a little and he feels, *Maybe I am getting old. It's a fact; no one seems to want me.* Being bounced around like that a few times has a way of taking the sparkle and enthusiasm out of a man.

Another man, in the middle years of his life, may have stayed with a company and become one of their vice-presidents. He has a beautiful office with his nameplate on the door, an executive secretary, a good income . . . and boredom. Where are the challenges? Vice-president of what? He could do his job in his sleep, "Let's see, how many more years till retirement . . . fifteen . . . twenty? How can I hold out that long? Maybe I'll get my resumé redone and look for a new job and a new challenge . . . But what if the president or the board of directors finds that I'm looking for another position? The last time a vice-president tried to look for a new position, someone found out and he was out just that quick."

The fear of change and the desire to feel protection and security inhibit this man from changing and growing. Instead he opts for security and boredom.

The Other Woman

Then there's the man who's been married for over twenty years and discovers that he's bored with his wife. This thought shakes him deeply. He has always been faithful to his wife.

He's been a good father, spending time with his children, going to ball games, playing with them. He's very proud of his children, and they are proud of their old man. He can't shake the strange and weird thoughts he's experiencing. He reassures himself that he has a good wife. She's been an excellent mother to the children—she's a good woman. So their sex life hasn't been the most exciting, and she's too tired to go out with him in the evening. He drops into a nice hotel after work and finds himself walking into the bar. Then the thought hits him, *Hey, I wonder if there's any action in this place.* He shakes himself, *That's not like me.* He sits down at the bar and orders a drink. *What am I doing here? I never stop in a bar going home from work.*

Pretty soon the bartender and he are shaking dice out of a cup to see who will pay for the next drink. He is joined by an attractive woman who joins in the dice throwing. Soon he and this woman are talking as if they are old friends. *Well,* he thinks, *maybe I haven't lost my sex appeal after all.* The whole evening is like being in a bubble, it's so unreal. He doesn't remember when he enjoyed talking to a woman so much. Soon they are dancing and ordering dinner. He did remember to call home and say he would be late. Yes, he would tell her later what came up.

He looks across the table at this woman who's at least ten years younger than he, and boy, is she coming on strong. After dinner and more dancing he's aware that he's a little rusty, but with her encouragement and praise, he starts cutting loose. Inside he feels a warm glow and he thinks, *I haven't had this much fun in years. All I've done is work, work, work and do for the family. Who could have believed that I would be out with this beautiful woman? Funny thing, I should feel guilty, but I don't. Is this really happening to me? I feel so different, so alive, so young. Something that makes a man feel that good can't be all that bad.*

In the weeks and months that follow, our middle-aged

Romeo loses fifteen pounds, mostly around the middle; he gets up early in the morning to go jogging; his hair grows longer. For the first time he goes to a hairstylist for the latest cut and to have the traces of gray removed. His wife is pleased that he is finally taking a renewed pride in his personal appearance, although she thinks his new clothes are a bit mod and the checks are a little bit garish for a man of his age; but he's never spent any money on himself, so let him buy whatever makes him feel good. He's even talking of buying a sports car—to save on gasoline, of course.

He acts differently at home. Sometimes he's thoughtful and kind, while at other times he's detached. His wife is puzzled by his moods, which range from a frantic high to a short-fused explosiveness and depression. When asked, "What's the matter?" he looks at her with fire in his eyes and snaps, "Just get off my back," then goes out for a night with the boys. *That's not like him*, she thinks, *but maybe it's just a phase he's going through. He doesn't even seem too interested in me sexually*, she thinks. *Well, maybe that's what it is like being middle-aged."*

Is Divorce the Answer?

For a man who never considered himself a swinger or a person to cheat on marriage, he is as surprised as anyone at his behavior. The other woman seems to know all the right things to say to him to make him feel good, and he is beginning to think that divorce is the answer. "I have my life to live, and frankly I don't know if I can spend all the rest of my years with my wife. She's a good mother, a good cook, and she keeps a beautiful home, but the other woman makes my life so exciting."

He finds himself daydreaming at work. Even his fellow

workers remark on how happy he seems to be, and what a wit he is.

"I have to talk to somebody before I go crazy." So our middle-aged Romeo seeks out, of course, an expert—a man who has been divorced for two years. "It's hard to bare your soul to another man, but Charlie, I've got to talk to someone."

So Charlie listens while he pours out his soul. Charlie understands exactly where he is and is very understanding. Finally Charlie speaks. "My friend, you're in trouble. You are like so many of us men who don't realize how vulnerable we are in the middle years and that some women are like sharks. They can smell a little drop of blood in the water, and they track a vulnerable man even before he knows what is happening."

"But Charlie, I think I'm in love with the woman. I have never felt so good, so full of life. I never knew that sex could be this great."

"I know," says Charlie, "it's hard to believe that you could be in love with two women at the same time, both of whom are different. But where to next?"

"Yeah, Charlie, I know my wife suspects something. She has that hurt look in her eyes, and she asked me if there was another woman. I snapped back with a guilty, 'No,' which, after twenty-two years, I know didn't fool her. She's always trusted and believed in me. We always felt so sorry for other couples our age who were getting divorced and said it would never happen to us. Then I spend an evening with my new love and I block out the reality that I'm married, that I have four kids. It's like a dream, a bubble that's my own reality. I'm messed up and confused. Charlie, if I divorce my wife, it will kill her. All she's done is be a good mother and a good wife. Where would she even go for a job? I couldn't just divorce my wife, and how would I face the four kids? Oh, I know they're older, but we've been so close. I'm afraid of their anger and rejection. What will I do, Charlie? What's happening to me?"

"Give yourself some time, and you'll get through the dangerous period. And remember, teenagers and middle-aged men are normally flaky."

Reordering Priorities

The middle years can create an identity crisis for a man who's never taken time to look at himself. He may start to philosophize about his own life. The introspection may help him to reorder his values and priorities in life.

The middle years of a man often bring his values and goals under the close scrutiny of self-examination. The heady optimism of youth has long been replaced with disillusionment and despair, not only about himself but for the world.

It can come as quite a jolt for the man who has considered himself a good Christian to realize that the great thrust of his energy, his life, his belief has been materialism, the god of mammon. Now as he surveys all he has gathered in material things, the symbols of his success, they seem so empty and bring no real joy. *Where is God as a priority in my life?* he asks himself. The answer is very clear—*Not very high.*

Even the man who has been active as a lay leader in his church begins to realize how tired he is of church committee meetings, ushering, stewardship drives, and all the business of the church. The deepest question he asks himself is "Why am I such a spiritual desert in spite of all my religious activity?" There is something missing in his life and such a man, like so many of us men in the middle years, is experiencing a crisis of faith, and he discovers a deep spiritual hunger for God. The psalmist expressed this longing for God in these words, "As the deer pants for water, so I long for you,

God. I thirst for God, the living God. Where can I find him
. . .?" (Psalms 42:1, 2).

In my own middle years I came to realize how deeply I
hungered to experience the presence of God. I wanted to go
beyond knowing what I believed about God, what I believed
about Jesus, and the Holy Spirit, to experience and know
God. This spiritual crisis of the middle years became a wonderful opportunity for me to grow spiritually.

Carl Jung wrote, "Among all my patients in the second half
of life—that is to say, over thirty-five—there has not been one
whose problem in the last resort was not that of finding a
religious outlook on life. It is safe to say that every one of
them fell ill because he had lost that which religions of every
age have given to their followers, and none of them has been
really healed who did not regain his outlook."[1]

Often he reaches out for companionship with his children
that he never had before, only to discover that they are moving out on their own, doing their own things, and there just
isn't time for dad. When children are young adults, going
their separate ways, it can be a very painful time for a man, as
he reexamines his life and who he is. He reaches out for his
wife, who may want to develop her own identity and find her
own way, because now she's free from spending so much of
her energy being a mother.

A Time of Opportunity

This pilgrimage can also prod and motivate a man to rediscover the opportunities of the middle years. I know that it has
been a powerful experience for me to look at myself, listen to
my pain, face the challenges of things I haven't wanted to see,
and then decide to grow. I've discovered that taking time to
do reflective thinking has helped me become more creative. I
find a new excitement and aliveness in my being. I'm fully

aware of the critical times that I've had to face and struggle through. In a way it's redundant of me to write of the dangers and opportunity of the middle years, because this book is the outgrowth of this period in my life.

If you are a man approaching the middle years, I hope you will realize that it's a time of danger, but opportunity. Take a good look at yourself. First, if you find that you're feeling sorry for yourself, blaming life and others for not being fair to you, remember, who said that life was fair? Put a period after yesterday. Examine your underutilized potential and begin to grow to new dimensions. The second half of life can be the best, because hopefully we don't have to repeat the mistakes of youth, and we have acquired some wisdom along the way. Set new goals for yourself as a person. Remember, the real problem of the second half of life is not hardening of the arteries, but hardening of the attitudes!

CHECKPOINT

1. What are the hazards of middle age?

2. When you need a support system, where do you go to find it?

3. Regardless of your chronological age, what age do you consider yourself? Why? Does the process of growing older bother you?

4. How do you cope with depression?

5. What major crisis (career changes, relocations, severe marital problems, etc.) have you faced in the past five years? Could you have handled them better?

6. What is meant by the statement, "The real problem of the second half of life is not hardening of the arteries, but hardening of the attitudes"?

7. What has happened to your spiritual life in the past five years?

8. Thinking of middle age as a time of danger and a time of opportunity, what two dangers and what two opportunities might be ahead of you in the immediate future?

—8—
WHEN A
MAN
IS
SICK

It's hard for a man to accept the vulnerability of being sick or disabled for any length of time. Most of us men suffer from what I call the p.i.e. syndrome (pride, ignorance, and ego) when faced with illness.

A man's false pride prevents him from admitting to himself any form of weakness or susceptibility to illness. Even when a man is sick, his pride is so stubborn that he fights going for medical help. Men are so proud, that it diminishes their masculinity to admit to any form of weakness. In looking back over twenty years of counseling, I would estimate that 80 percent of the people who came to me for counseling were women, or teenagers who were forced to see me. A common attitude exhibited by men, when their marriage is in serious trouble, is to heartily recommend that the wife go for therapy. He believes it may do his wife some good, but that he doesn't need therapy. That would be tantamount to admitting that there might be something wrong with him.

Over the years of marriage counseling I developed an effective strategy to get the husband involved. At first I believed a wife when I asked if she had asked her husband to be a part of the counseling and she would assure me that she had pleaded with the husband and he had emphatically said no. I soon discovered that the wife often assumed her husband would not agree to marriage counseling as a couple. So I would call the husband at work, while his wife was in my presence, and say, for example, "John, this is Ken Olson, did you know your wife was talking to me about your troubled marriage?"

Most often I would hear a shocked, "No, I didn't know she was seeking counseling."

"I asked her if you wanted to be a part of the counseling, but was told you had said no. One of my ground rules for marriage counseling is that each person can only speak for him- or herself. Do you want your wife to speak for you?"

In about every instance the answer was no, and the next request was for an appointment. I realize now that I was using the man's pride to set up the counseling.

False Pride

The programming of a man makes it difficult for him to admit weakness, sickness, or anything that exposes his vulnerability. When a man is sick and has to be incapacitated for a period of time, he often feels guilty—surely this can't be happening to him. A friend of mine said that when he is sick he feels so guilty that he keeps taking his temperature to reassure himself that he's actually sick enough to stay home from work. A man's pride may also cause him to exaggerate verbally the pain he's experiencing, to say to his family, if you realize how much pain I am in, then I won't feel so guilty about being sick. There are other reasons for talking about pain, which I will discuss later.

A man's pride is demonstrated by his belief that he will always be healthy. He's invincible and nothing like a little sickness can ever slow him down. This pride demands that he ignore or belittle the warning signals his brain and body are giving him. That little pain in the chest is just a little indigestion that a few Alka-Seltzers, and maybe some Valium, will chase away. Besides he doesn't have time to go to his physician for a checkup. If the warning signals persist, this man may even increase the pace of his life, take on more responsibilities as if to prove to himself that he is invulnerable to sickness; and then he collapses, to no one's surprise but his own.

The average American male is overweight, including yours truly, but only about 15 to 20 percent of the overweight people on diets are men. I think when an overweight man looks in the mirror he doesn't see himself, but some other thin young man. Even when he suffers from "lap-belta," meaning his stomach laps over his belt, he may see a Greek god in the mirror. So many of us men suffer not only from false pride, but ignorance. Some of our ignorance is our fault, and some of the responsibility for our ignorance belongs to the medical profession.

I was at a friend's home just after he returned from a complete physical. He told me his doctor had said he was in great health. That afternoon he died of a heart attack! The medical profession is trained to be a disease-oriented profession; consequently, little, if any, training is given to physicians on what health is and how to keep a person healthy. The World Health Organization's definition of *health* is "a state of complete physical, mental and social well-being of the individual and not the mere absence of disease." My friend's heart disease took a long time to develop, and it didn't appear just that afternoon. There were symptoms a long time before the heart attack.

"Effective" medicine and dentistry, which treats only the symptoms and the effects of disease, is not very effective, but it is very expensive. Medicine has performed miracles in eliminating communicable diseases, developing miraculous surgical techniques and medical technological developments. The challenge of today is from the wear and tear of time damage caused by a life of too much stress.

The Effect of Stress

Stress is a way the body responds to stress-activating signals from our environment or our thoughts. The body responds through the hypothalamus, the autonomic nervous system: the pituitary and adrenal glands release hormones that prepare a person for meeting a challenge. The response of stress is not bad, because it activates the body to meet a challenge. Too little stimulation from the external world on the brain can also be very harmful.

Stress becomes distress when the person is in a state of prolonged stress without any chance to return to normal functioning and to renew bodily resources. Too much stress for too long causes the body to continue to react as if it were threatened long after the actual stress-activating event has occurred. When stress becomes distress, the body will begin experiencing some tissue damage. We know that the stress response can change a person's endocrine output, his brain activity, weaken the disease resistors in the immune system, alter the blood supply and blood pressure, as well as the rate of respiration and the digestive processes. A person will unconsciously select an organ or particular part of the body to focus this distress; and thus, symptoms will develop, messages that his life is out of balance and he's not effectively dealing with the stress in his life.

What I am suggesting is a holistic approach to health and sickness. The simple disease model that sickness is always the result of a single factor or germ is inadequate. What I think about, brood about, and desire about my life will affect my physical well-being. If I am depressed and filled with anxiety, then the hypothalamus will send out messages to other parts in my body. This can result in tissue damage. If I carry around a degree of muscle tension, this will activate the hypothalamus, which will produce emotions of depression and anxiety. There is some truth in saying to a person it's all in his head because that is where his hypothalamus resides. It is, however, poor practice of medicine to tell a person that the pain in his stomach, which is very real, is all in his head, meaning that he is a hypochondriac.

Conventional medicine, with its yearly physical, considers a person well if he has no symptoms and falls within specified normal ranges in diagnostic tests. However, this "well" person might smoke two packs of cigarettes a day, drink too much alcohol, be overweight, eat poorly, with a diet of too much sugar, do no exercise, and be bottled up emotionally and depressed. From my point of view, and others', this person is sick and is a high risk for serious, if not fatal, illness.

Dr. John C. McCamy and James Presley write in *Human Life Styling:* "Isolating each risk factor, we find that at age forty a man has five times more chance of giving himself a heart attack if he is overweight. If he does absolutely no exercise, his dangers are six times those of a man who takes a short walk every day. Those who regularly do aerobic exercises—sustained walking, running, swimming, and biking may lower their risks as much as *one hundred times*. On the other hand, smoking increases your risks from four to eight times. And the person with a three-hundred-milligram blood-cholesterol reading has ten times the risk of a person with a two-hundred reading."

They go on to discuss the relationship between heart disease and emotional stress. "The overachievers, those who set goals for themselves and are rigid and not relaxed, have an eighty percent correlation with heart attacks."[1]

Dr. Flanders Dunbar, in 1943, attempted to match up personality traits and emotional problems with various physical disorders. Among the heart attack patients were many highly trained professionals and self-made men who seemed to have difficulty sharing their responsibilities and getting along with others. The more stressful their life became, the unhappier they were, and the unhappier they became, the harder they worked. Dunbar said their most striking characteristic was "compulsive striving." "They would rather die than fail."

Loss of Control

A man's ego can be a killer . . . pride, ignorance, and ego, the p.i.e. syndrome. When a man becomes ill, is forced to be inactive for a period of time, one of the most common reactions is "Why did I have to get sick?" His emotional reaction often is the delusion that he's the first man ever to be so sick and disabled. The reality of his vulnerability to sickness is viewed as a massive assault on his ego, and he may be very angry and irritable with the whole world. Nothing anyone can do for him is right, soon enough, or helpful. Now please bear with me, and remember not all men react this way. Maybe it's a distinct minority.

After a time of raging at his illness, a man may withdraw and become quietly depressed. There can be a marked personality change, especially if there is a lengthy period of incapacitation and recuperation, as with a heart attack. It may be impossible to keep down in bed a compulsively driven man who has had a heart attack, then been released from the hospital and told to go home, take it easy, and do nothing.

Maybe the advice to do nothing is dangerous. The hardest thing for most of us to do is nothing, but for a compulsive, driven man, doing nothing can be fatal. Dr. Peter Ortiz believes "that the idle mind is the cradle of stress." It would be better medicine if a man who had plenty of time on his hands writes his thoughts down on paper or records them on cassettes. That is the time to get his emotions outside and not bottle them up for another explosion. Maybe in time he can enjoy reading, writing his own autobiography, looking at his goals in life, or whatever, but he must be able to do something more than nothing. If not, this once dynamic, energetic man may become quiet and passive, and nothing will interest him anymore. He may want to be mothered, have people feel sorry for him, and yet resent any attempt at mothering or pity. He could crawl inside his head, so to speak, and worry about what's going to happen to his career, how the bills will be paid. Then comes the frightening realization of how tenuous life is and how easily a person can be replaced. He sees his wife scurrying around the home, making decisions he never thought she could make.

The loss of control over his life is the most devastating blow to a man's ego. A man who is used to being in charge and making decisions is now faced with something beyond his control—illness. It makes a man feel of little importance. He feels about as useful as a man who spits in the desert to end a long drought. In a "disposable society" a man can, at this point, feel he is disposable and unimportant. In this period of withdrawal and depression, a man may give in to helplessness and, without realizing it, give in to illness and incapacitation. He may develop a depressive picture of himself as a sick, weak man who has given up hope that he will ever be well again.

A goal of sickness and weakness can become a self-fulfilling prophecy which will eventually bring death. Efforts to get such a man back on his feet will be resisted, because he doesn't believe he will ever be well again, and all this fussing and effort to get him to do something is just a waste of time. Now he's suffering from a massive case of self-pity. Even pain will be magnified. His general weakness is living proof that he hasn't the strength. The more he talks about his pain, his aches, how tasteless the food is, the more he believes himself to be a man doomed to illness and disability. In short, he has made the decision not to get well. At this point he needs to be confronted.

Participate in the Healing Process

Healing resides in each person, and without the decision to take personal responsibility for wanting to get well there most likely will be no healing, or at best a prolonged recovery. It is essential that a person focus his mind on the powers of healing so he can be an active participant in the healing process rather than a passive, irresponsible patient.

I have had little personal experience with being sick, so I can't share with you how I coped. I'm confident that almost everything I have written about the vulnerability of a man when he is sick would not apply to me if I ever became ill and had to spend a period of time recovering. I'm not that kind of man, and besides, I just don't see myself as ever being sick. My ego wouldn't stand for it!

Since I can't report firsthand, I have asked a friend of mine, our pastor, Jim Lundeen, to tell you about his feelings when he was laid up with a slipped disc in his back for over a month. It all began when he swung a bat at a softball game last summer and felt the pain. In December he had to go to the hospital to be put into traction.

Oh! My Aching Back

There is no pain so great that it could incapacitate me—certainly not at this point in my life. Thirty-seven years old, always active, athletic, in basically good health. Why, no injury could toss me flat on my back for any extended period of time! That's something that happens to someone else—to those not as fit as I am. Oh, I have my little aches, pains, and sicknesses, but nothing could befall me that would keep me from my appointed duties for more than a day or two—surely not now—or so I thought.

Here I am writhing on the floor. This is so out of character for me—it's a disorienting experience. This can't really be happening to me. My back feels paralyzed—and my right leg is on fire, the calf knotted in spasms of pain. I thought it was just a pulled muscle—but what if I have really messed up my back to the point where it will never be the same again—where *I* will never be the same again? I can't bear such a thought. My very existence depends on my motor ability. And now I can't move without—well, for all practical purposes, I can't move, period! Who—what does that make me? A big fat *zero*, that's what! Why can't I just 'tough it out' like I've always done before? I don't know why, I just know I can't. I've got to do something to get relief.

The hospital? But that's for people who are really sick, I've just got this pain. What a terrible, incapacitating pain. Okay, the hospital it is. But it seems so strange. How often I've stood at another's bed and secretly wished for the opportunity to take a break from my 'go-go' type of life and jump into a hospital bed for a little rest. But now the opportunity is at hand—in fact, is being forced upon me—I don't want to go. I don't want to give up my freedom. I don't want to make myself vulnerable to some nurse poking my body with needles. It's degrading—dehumanizing. What am I doing going to the hospital? Why, there's not that much wrong with me.

Oh, that leg hurts! Can't you hurry up with those questions, lady, so I can get upstairs to bed! Of course I've got insurance. What do you think I am—irresponsible or something? Lady, I've got to go to bed. Can you ask my wife? She's the only one in our family who's capable of carrying on now anyway. But is she capable enough? What if I'm permanently crippled? How would my family ever make it? I feel the panic of desperation rising within me. I've got to get better. If I don't, I can't really justify my own existence. I'll never allow myself to be a drain on society, most certainly not my family.

The pain has subsided. Maybe I'm okay now. I'll bet I am.

See—you can't keep me down for more than a day or two. I feel pretty good. This is fun to lay around and get all this attention. A fella deserves a day like this every once in a while. King Jim with all these servants to do my bidding, "My lady, could you get me a cup of coffee?" I've served others plenty and "turnabout's fair play," isn't it?

"Hey, doc, we've played this game long enough haven't we? Let me go home—I've got to get going—I've got a job to do— I'm beginning to feel guilty. What am I doing lying here? I've got no right to spend my days like this. Others are depending on me. Things are going to get all goofed up at work if I'm not around. It will crumble without me. Yes, I'm *that* important! . . . What kind of husband and father am I turning out to be? There's Ruth stuck with all the responsibilities of home and family. Come on, *back*, shape up, so I can get out of here and relieve myself of all the guilt I'm feeling. Get out of here—what a joke. I can't even relieve myself *physically* without pain and without the degradation of the bed pan! And now the doctors say I need more time in the hospital. I can't believe it. I'm young, strong, and invincible. Why can't I stand on that leg for more than a few minutes? Why can't I? I want to know. Tell me, God, why can't I? Why's the pain so excruciating? What if it never *goes* away? I'm getting angry! I'm getting afraid! I'm getting depressed! It's not fair. Why would God permit such a thing to happen to me? I won't be a cripple all my life—worth nothing to anyone. If I can't be a total man, I choose to be no man at all. I'll show you, God, for doing this to me! I'm not going to be a full-time burden on Ruth. Why, this could go on for years! Maybe Ruth should "unload" me now before I drag her down too far. No, God, no— maybe she will!

Ed and Keith tell me things are going fine on the job. What is that supposed to mean? They're trying to tell me something, aren't they? Perhaps things are "going fine" *because* of my absence. The worst reality of all really hits me like a ton of bricks. I'm not indispensable at all. I smile to hear that others are picking up the ball in my absence, but down deep I resent that fact. It hurts to know that the place will survive my departure. Maybe I'll be *asked* to resign. I've got to get better soon or I'll be out on my ear! I feel so anxious—I break into a cold sweat as I write these lines. They don't need me or even like me at work, do they? How could I have been so foolish to think otherwise? How come so few have come to see me—or called—or sent cards? That proves it—I am nothing. I am the ugly, unnecessary, insignificant Aldonza, and all because of this back! What about all those I put myself out for? Where are they? Don't they care? Doesn't anyone care? If not, then I don't care either.

I'm ready to give up. If only the back hadn't given up the ghost. Then I could have shielded myself from uncovering the awful reality about my life. When you lie flat on your back, your soft belly of vulnerability is exposed. Do you suppose lying flat on your back also serves another purpose? I thought I was so self-sufficient, but lying flat on my back totally helpless, I find myself looking up. Do you suppose there's a message there someplace?

Time, which has always been so important to me, means nothing here. Time has meaning only within the framework of freedom, and here I have lost my freedom. I am a prisoner. Others make my decisions, and I am as a child—a robot. Is this Wednesday or Friday? Who knows? More importantly, who cares? Is it 4:00 P.M. or noon? What difference does it make? But get my paper to me *before* I shave, and give me some time to ponder tomorrow's menu. Those are the important decisions and priorities for me now. They're the *only* decisions and priorities for me now. The man with the key priorities—the maker of important decisions is reduced to subsimple issues. How tenuous is the lot of the human. One "bop" in the back and so much of the superstructure of my life is exposed as a meaningless sham. Who am I really? What is "me"? What of me is worthwhile no matter what happens to my back? What makes a man a man? What is really important about life?

I want to thank Jim for sharing his private thoughts on his period of illness and the wait for healing. He's doing fine now, but as much as he loves softball, I wonder if he will swing another bat.

I personally hate the thought of being sick and incapacitated, so I have decided to stay healthy. I realize my most valuable possession is my health.

CHECKPOINT

1. What is the p.i.e. syndrome? Does it relate to you and your attitude toward your health?

2. Are there changes that you could make in your lifestyle that could benefit your health? What is keeping you from making those changes?

3. During times in your life when you have been physically ill, how was your behavior and outlook on life affected?

4. Look again at Pastor Jim Lundeen's reaction to his hospitalization. List the various emotional and psychological reactions that he felt.

—9—

DO I HAVE
TO DIE
WHEN
I RETIRE?

Insurance companies have statistical data which would seem to indicate that men whose only goal is to retire die within eighteen months after achieving that goal.

In talking with retired men, you find a common problem—that suddenly they feel they have nothing to look forward to, or as one man put it: "When I was working, I always looked forward to my weekends and summer vacations, and I don't have that to look forward to anymore." A friend mentioned to a recently retired man that now he could do all the things he'd always wanted to do, to which the newly retired man replied, "All I ever wanted to do was work."

It seems that too many men become one-dimensional, men whose major life energies and self-worth are incorporated solely in their work. A woman asked my help with her husband who had tried to commit suicide the previous weekend. He was sixty-five and had worked eighteen hours a day, seven days a week. He had a heart attack at sixty-two and was forced to sell his corporation. His wife explained that he was a good, honest man, and he had generously given her close to thirty thousand dollars to spend on Indian jewelry and art during the past year.

As gently as I could, I warned her that her husband was at a very high risk for another suicide attempt. I asked how he was doing in the hospital, and to my shock she said, "Oh, he made such a fuss about being in the hospital, and especially on the psychiatric floor, that the doctor discharged him today because he was such a difficult patient. I don't think I could convince him to come see you either."

I quickly told her to have her husband rehospitalized because if this wasn't done, he would again try to take his life. He refused to go to a hospital, and two days later he committed suicide. His whole life was his work. When his work ended, so did his life.

There is a fantasy that magically a new life will begin once a man retires. What actually develops is the problem of dealing with unstructured time and boredom. I asked one man what he and his wife did for fun. "Fun, let's see?" Neither of them could remember what they did for fun.

"What would you like to do for fun?" I asked.

"Oh, travel a lot," came the quick reply.

"But do you travel now?"

"No, we can't afford to travel now, we are going to do a lot of traveling when I retire."

"If you don't have money to travel with now, where will the money suddenly come from?"

"Social Security?"

The traveling you'll do then is to the drugstore for your prescriptions after your trip to the doctor's office. Maybe once in a while you both can spend a thrilling afternoon people-watching in a big shopping mall. Don't wait to travel or live. Men who wait too long only provide insurance money for their widows to travel to Hawaii or Europe with other widows.

DO I HAVE TO DIE WHEN I RETIRE?

I don't like the word *retire*. Retire from what? Give up a job so you can play a game of checkers or golf while waiting for death? Retirement carries the message of getting old. How does a person accept being old in an age that worships youth? A few generations ago the young looked to the older people for the wisdom and knowledge they gathered in life. Then when we became urbanized, older people were out of place and old-fashioned. With the knowledge explosion, parents felt out of step and out of place in a world of constant change and shock, and somehow the children were at home in this world.

A Negative Image

To be old came to be a dreaded experience, because a person felt cast aside and useless. We began to develop pictures and beliefs about how people act when they are "old."

"I am sixty years old. I should start to be forgetful, totter a little when I walk, talk only about things of long ago, believe I'm too old to learn anything new; after all, 'you can't teach an old dog new tricks.' I should lose interest in sex, be careful not to strain myself physically, and generally act bored and useless."

If that's the picture, the goal, and the programming a person accepts, then he will act in those ways, live up to his belief of how an old person should act, and he will reach his goal. Recent research on aging, however, shows that people can continue to learn new information and knowledge. The brain doesn't suddenly go downhill. If an older person is forgetful, it's most likely because he doesn't pay attention, or he's decided not to listen and think. At any age it's almost impossible to remember if you fail to listen and think. Sometimes all that is needed is to have the wax cleaned out of the ears.

Sexual activity can continue into the seventies and eighties.

Now I know how thrilled some of the women are to hear this news. A person who takes good care of his body with proper nutrition and exercise and who learns how to live with stress successfully can have an active physical life.

The boredom of older people isn't so much the result of aging as it is the result of a loss of enthusiasm and interest in life. People are boring, not life. Boredom is as big a problem with some teenagers as it is with older people. The problem is suffering from hardening of the attitudes, not hardening of the arteries. Some recent experiments have provided us with fresh ideas about how people should live in a nursing home. The experiment was a simple one of providing the residents with a limited cocktail hour before dinner. The people had something to look forward to, and they remembered how they used to be alive instead of vegetating in a nursing home. They changed for the better. The gloomy atmosphere of the nursing home was gone, all because there was something more to life than a sleeping pill.

Tapping Your Creative Potential

I have decided that I will not be an "old man." I plan to live to ninety and die young. I am always going to be open to life and keep on learning something new, so when I finally die, I might be an educated man with some wisdom. I'm using the time to set some growth goals for the rest of my life.

The second half of life can be very exciting. George Burns was in his eighties when he won his first Oscar, for his performance in *The Sunshine Boys*. He talked of the creative potential in the older adult: "When you get old enough to be young again."

Old people are discovering the rich untapped talent and potential in themselves. They are setting new goals. Remember, if you believe you are through at sixty-two, then you are through, but only because you believed it. That became your goal. You don't have to lose your sense of adventure and belief in yourself. Use the wisdom you have acquired through the years of living. Don't put a premature period on your life or let anyone else do that to you. Have fun with music, writing, art, or whatever. Go out and find people to love.

On a talk show in Dallas, an older woman talked with me about where she could get training to help the elderly in nursing homes to redevelop interests in life and learning. We discussed courses she could take in community colleges. Her last question really blew my mind. "Do you think these nursing homes have entrances constructed so I could get inside with my wheelchair?" That's the attitude toward life I have been talking about.

I realize I have sounded very positive, and maybe at times naive, about growing old. I just realized that these words I have written were mainly for my benefit, to help me set goals. I doubt if I will ever completely retire. I wonder how these words of mine will sound to me fifteen years from now. I promise I will try to listen to my own advice. I don't like the thought, or picture, of my being in a nursing home. I'm not so much afraid of death—but the process of dying, or being an invalid, troubles me deeply.

CHECKPOINT

1. What plans have you made for retirement?

2. What do you think you will be doing in your retirement years?

3. What new things would you like to learn or do after retirement?

RELATIONSHIPS

part four

—10—
IT'S NOT GOOD FOR MAN TO BE ALONE

There it is again!
A twinge of pain?
Forget it. It will go away
In the business of my day.
I've places to go and things to do . . .
A round of meetings with entrepreneurs.
Planes to catch and taxis to hail,
I have life by the tail.
But what is this painful wail?
From the depths of me I ache.
It greets me when I wake.
Even in a crowded room of people
I can hear a haunting toll
          from a church bell steeple.
There's nothing wrong with me.
I'm a success as anyone can see.
I—I hurt. I feel an emptiness.

This feeling, is it loneliness?
Loneliness?
I'm married with children, three,
Yet at times I feel so alone
Maybe it's time to come down from my throne.
It's not good for man to be alone.

I was sitting on another airplane as I wrote those words. The extensive traveling I have done in the past few years has provided me with ample time to be alone and experience the deep pain of loneliness. Do I get lonely only because I'm away from home, or is my being away from home bringing to the surface a much deeper loneliness and hunger for relationships? I wonder how many of us men ever stop long enough to be still and hear the ache of loneliness from deep within. I know, at times, that I have filled my life with more than enough to do so I haven't had the time to feel that pain. In quiet times I sense a restless, unsatisfied hunger deep within me for intimacy and dialogue, but maybe my masks, my pride, my fears of rejection inhibit the expression of these needs.

It might seem strange that I should be writing about loneliness when I have been so involved with people through the ministry, counseling, and conducting seminars, but all of us experience loneliness. We greet each other, but so seldom meet.

A Lonely Occupation

While the years I served as a pastor were filled with people, the ministry is a very lonely occupation. I tried in vain to break down the barriers, but there was always a wall separating pastor and parishioner. This loneliness was especially painful for Jeannie. She did have to play the typical role of the minister's wife, but still it was hard and lonely. You could really feel set apart from other people if you went to a New

Year's Eve party and felt the uncomfortable silence after you were introduced as Pastor Ken and Jeannie Olson.

It was a joy to have intern pastors from the seminary assigned to work with me and the congregation for a year. Each man became special to me. A deep relationship was developed so that each man, when he felt safe, could let his hair down and express his deepest thoughts and feelings. I miss having that type of relationship with a man now. There are some things I could share with a man that I don't share with Jeannie.

Away From Home

When I first began to travel extensively, I was so excited and anxious to experience this glamorous life. I was able to visit places that I had only dreamed of before. When Jeannie could accompany me and we could spend a few extra days seeing the places, it was especially great. But most of the time I traveled alone. What I saw was another airport, another hotel, or motel conference room filled with people I didn't know. I would do my best to put on a good show, then pack my bags and fly home exhausted and suffering from jet lag.

The glamor faded fast, especially when it was time for another dinner alone. I would stare at the empty chair across the table, order a fine meal, and in less than five minutes, the whole experience would be over. *Now what should I do since that didn't take much time? Should I go back to my room which smells of stale cigarettes, cigar smoke, and dirt and turn on the TV? And if I don't go to sleep watching TV, maybe I should go back down to the lounge and listen to some music, lift my spirits.* Chances are I hear some songs that magnify my loneliness—like "One is the Lonelist Number," or "Alone Again, Naturally," or "Eleanor Rigby"—"All the lonely people, where do they all come from?" Here I am, a long way from home in a lounge in

Excitement City and my eyes scan the room. I meet a pair of eyes that are also looking around the room . . . a traveling salesman surveying the scene with drink and cigarette in hand. *Boy, this is really living.*

The worst travel ordeal is when the publisher puts you on the road for a month for a book promotion. The experiences are such that you promise you'll never write another book for fear that you'll have to go out and promote it. Every author can tell you war stories of blurry eyes, blurry days, foul-ups in scheduling of radio and television shows, of weariness that is beyond fatigue. To be an author it helps to be able to live with an irregular life-style and sleeping pattern. You must be able to miss meals and have a cast-iron stomach for all that "mountain grown" coffee, plus superhuman bladder control.

Loneliness is a very painful experience. I realized that I was haunted with moments of loneliness even when I was at home. Had I become so accustomed to being alone that I found it difficult to relate? Could it be that in the best of marriages there is loneliness? Albert Schweitzer described it with these words, "We are all so much together but we are all dying of loneliness."

One very bright moonlit night I was flying over Texas and looking at the small homes. I began to wonder what was going on in each of them. How many couples were quarreling? How many homes were filled with love? How many people were living out another boring, lonely evening in front of the TV set? The awareness of the possibility of so many lonely lives in homes spread out below me was overwhelming. Leo Rosten's words came to me. "Everyone is lonely at the bottom, and cries out to be understood, but we can never really understand anyone else. We remain part strangers even to those who love us." As we flew on through the moonlit night, the words and haunting melody of a hymn we sing at the folk worship service kept running through my mind:

IT'S NOT GOOD FOR MAN TO BE ALONE

Lonely voices crying in the city,
Lonely voices sounding like a child.
Lonely voices come from busy people
Too disturbed to stop a little while.
Lonely voices haunt my memory.[1]

A Life Never Fully Shared

Loneliness is an experience common to all of us, yet, by its very nature, it is a profoundly private reality, full of raw sensitivity and pain. The pain of loneliness can become so intense that we inwardly cry out, "Doesn't anybody hear me hurting? How could anyone not see this loneliness!" But they don't. I think that somewhere along the line, in the experience of loneliness, each of us becomes aware that we are solitary, unique individuals, whose deepest fear and hopes may never really be fully shared with another person.

Loneliness seems to be in the air in our contemporary society. We have become so mobile, so transient, so preoccupied with our own personal life-styles that we seldom have time for others. One of the saddest occurrences of our times is the disappearance of the extended family living close by and of friendships. How many close friends do you have? How many new friends have you recently cultivated?

Clark Moustakas writes in his book, *Loneliness*:

Why is it that so many individuals in modern life yearn for a fundamental relatedness to others, but are unable to experience it? What is it that stands between man and man? Why is it that in face to face meetings, man is unable to be spontaneous, truthful and direct with his fellow man? What makes so many people today act in opposition to their own natures, to their own desires and requirements? Why is self-estrangement and fear of loneliness so common in modern life?[2]

Why Settle for Superficial Relationships?

Loneliness will always be a barrier until we face our own alienation, look at our values or lack of values, find out a reason for being, and have the courage to throw away our masks, reveal what we think, feel, fear, hope, and dream to another person. In John Powell's book *Why Am I Afraid to Tell You Who I Am?* are these poignant words: "Most of us feel that others will not tolerate much emotional honesty in communication. We would rather defend our dishonesty on the grounds that it might hurt others, and having rationalized our phoniness into nobility, we settle for superficial relationships."[3]

As I experienced my own loneliness, I became aware of how much more loneliness Jeannie had had to live with because of my life-style, especially when I was on the road lecturing. At times I never even thought about her being alone and the void it created in her life. And then, when I would come home from a trip, she wanted companionship and wanted to know what had happened on the trip. I would say, "Oh, don't bother me now. I'm too tired. We'll talk about it later." I was always putting her off until I could squeeze her into my world. I realize now that my illusion of myself as being such a neat and sensitive husband was a fraud. I thought I was aware and sensitive of a woman's needs, but when my loneliness forced me to examine my own needs, it blatantly pointed out my ability to lock out Jeannie into her own loneliness.

Maybe this is true for all men. I had to become aware of my own self-centeredness before I recognized my belief that my world was more important than my wife's needs. I was first, and somewhere down the line my wife stood waiting. I see how I controlled our relationship by putting her off to suit my needs—my timing. I needed to grow, develop, and become more aware and sensitive in our relationship, and this had become a goal for me. It's funny how, after all these years,

I've wondered at times, "What could be bugging Jeannie?" Finally my swift, keen, analytical mind figured it out. It was me.

Painfully, loneliness can help us remember our basic need of relationships. It isn't loneliness that kills us, but our reaction to loneliness. Loneliness can drive us to grow and be open to others as human beings with the same relationship needs.

"And the Lord God said, 'It isn't good for man to be alone. I will make a companion for him, a helper suited to his needs' " (Genesis 2:18).

Broken Hearts

It is not only not good for man to be alone, but it is also hazardous to his health. The older a man becomes, the more vulnerable he is to the devastation of the loss of a wife through death. I have often wondered whether most men have such a fear of being alone in their old age that they program themselves to die first so they won't be so helpless and alone.

People actually do die of broken hearts although I have never seen a death certificate which listed the cause of death as a broken heart, grief, or loneliness. Colin Parkes, in his book *Bereavement: Studies in Grief in Adult Life*, points out the vulnerability of a person who has experienced a deep, personal loss.

The increased mortality rate among the grief-stricken, Parkes writes, is especially high during the first six months after the loss of a loved one through death. In 75 percent of the cases Parkes studied the cause of death was coronary thrombosis or arteriosclerosis.[4]

In his book *The Broken Heart* James Lynch reports that the premature death rates for divorced, widowed, and single men from cardiovascular disease were two to three times higher than for married men.[5] The single man is three times as prone to nervous breakdown as single women or married men.[6]

Marriage Underrated

We live in an incredible, unbelievable world of science and technology. It seems that with all our scientific skill and technology we can solve any problem, except the problem of human relationships, like marriage and the family. I think our knowledge of marital and family relationships is still in the Stone Age. It seems paradoxical that with the expanding knowledge of the universe, we progress rapidly backward in our ability to understand and solve the basic problems of human relationships—for example, how to live and discover the potential within a committed relationship called marriage.

It's hard to figure out whether it's my age, the times in which we live, the number of years we've been married, or all of the above and more, but I've become much more aware of divorce. When Jeannie and I were first married, divorce was discussed in the hushed, distasteful terms of tragic failure. Now it seems that divorce is like a virus. It's in the air. I have shared with others the same anxiety over the increasing number of divorces among our best friends. Marriages with a history of eighteen, twenty, twenty-five, even thirty years are now ending in divorce. In Maricopa County, Arizona, the rate is such that we have a divorce granted for every marriage license issued.

All of a sudden the goal of a lasting marriage has changed for many people into a belief that staying in the same marriage isn't really desirable. The media bombards us with talk of serial marriages.

Women are encouraged to set themselves free from the bondage of the housewife and mother role. I find as I listen to some of them, that even though they chose to get married, they now resent being housewives or mothers. And it's the husband's fault and not their choosing at all. They want to be everything at the same time. They want to have a career, they want to be a wife, they want to be a mother, and they want to be the complete person in all those areas. To be less than that is to be a failure. Such programming sows seeds of discontent about marriage and "gives permission" for divorce. "Everybody's doing it so why don't I join in the final reprieve to be a swinger and express my individuality?" Dr. John Money of Johns Hopkins University boldly asserts: "I would like to see more varieties of life-style. We don't need the idea of monogamous marriage for life—till death do us part. Death used to part us much sooner than it does now."[7]

The Endangered American Family

The traditional family in America is experiencing such rapid and disturbing changes that I wonder if it is now an endangered species. Historians warn us that if the traditional family unit of the family fails, the nation will soon fall into rapid decline.

Urie Bronfenbrenner, one of the world's leading authorities on child development, writes:

> That the family is the central institution comes as no surprise to most anthropologists, ethnic patriarchs, or social historians because the family is the only social institution that is present in every single village, tribe, people, or nation-state we know throughout history. But that the family is the core institution in every society may startle and annoy many contemporary Americans. For most of us it is the individual that is the chief social unit. It's always the individual, with "the government" a weak second. The family is not currently a social unit we value or support.[8]

There is an "I-dolatry" in our land that is destroying our nation. The Communist party of the Soviet Union could not have developed a better plan to destroy the United States from within than what we are doing all by ourselves. Maybe we should change our national anthem to "I Did It My Way."

It really isn't good for a man, or anyone, to live alone. I'm very cognizant of how much I need a wife to share my life and create our memories. Someone who loves, cares, and forgives me. A person who knows my deepest secrets and still accepts me as I am. I need a wife with whom I can communicate at a deep level. I am very much aware that, "One man is no man."

CHECKPOINT

1. When was the last time you felt really lonely?

2. What circumstances contribute to your feelings of loneliness?

3. Do you feel that if you could communicate better, you would be less lonely?

4. Why are there so many divorces of people who have been married for twenty or thirty years?

5. What are you doing to establish meaningful friendships with other men?

6. What are you doing to establish a meaningful friendship with your wife?

—11—
WHY IS
IT SO
HARD
TO TALK?

The biggest complaint a wife has about her husband is that he just doesn't talk to her enough.

A man's biggest complaint about his wife is that she doesn't want to have sex often enough.

It has occurred to me that these two fundamental needs are related to each other. Not enough discourse leads to less intercourse.

Before marriage a man may have been an exciting, impressive, witty conversationalist with his woman, and this can be very impressive. He's clever at small talk, and soon a woman feels they have so many common interests that he would be a good husband; so she decides that he should marry her. After the marriage there isn't a noticeable change, but rather it's a subtle, gradual change in the husband-wife communication patterns. She waits for him to be open and communicative, and maybe what she gets is criticism for not doing something correctly, anger for bugging him about something, or she's put off with, "Not now, can't you see I'm busy." This shuts the wife out. Then, one evening when having dinner at a lovely restaurant with their best friends, she sees the old spark and witty conversationalist in her husband blossom forth again as he talks so vivaciously and animatedly to the other man's wife. Now, is the wife jealous? Maybe. Confused and resentful? Yes. But more than that, troubled. "Why can't he talk that way to me? He used to be so much fun to talk with, and now he's either too tired or watching the idiot box; and when he does speak, it's in short, declarative statements such as: 'Give me a beer.' 'Let's go to bed.' 'What's for dinner?' 'Where's my blue shirt?' "

"There are none so blind as those who will not see." I confess now that I'm guilty of not being as effective a communicator or listener with my wife as I should be. But I didn't see that before. I believed I wasn't guilty. I used silence as an excuse for my noninvolvement, by saying, "Well, I'm doing some thinking."

Like every person I have a public me and a private me, and both are me. When I'm giving a talk, conducting a seminar, or appearing on television or radio, I am *on*. I'm witty, charming, warm, sensitive, and communicative. I expend an enormous amount of emotional and mental energy, and that context determines my behavior. For those of you who know me, the public me, I think you can understand how hard it is for me to share with you, in this book, the private me. I'm human enough to recognize that I enjoy people's admiration and appreciation. I don't like to tarnish my public me by relating to you that in another context—with my wife and my children— there is a private me that is also very human and very fallible.

It doesn't meet Jeannie's needs for me to say, when she has requested communication, "Look, honey, I gave it all at work." She doesn't buy that anymore. Sometimes Jeannie would say, "Hey, Kenny, how 'bout sparkling a little for us at home? Can't you save a little of your charisma and energy for those of us who live with you?" Now, when she puts it that way, it does get my attention and causes me to think.

Why is it so hard for me to talk to Jeannie? Have twenty-five years allowed me to slip into a bad rut? I sometimes recognize that I was programmed not to speak. "Don't rock the boat . . . peace at any price." I didn't see my father and mother as great communicators. For many years my father was working out of town, gone for months at a time. My early programming was that married people don't talk too much; but that's no excuse for me. I know better.

Boring . . . Who, Me?

One night Jeannie asked me why it was so difficult to communicate, even make small talk. Small talk isn't just small talk, it's a way of recognizing the existence of the other. I had the courage to say, "Well, maybe I don't talk as much to you as I should because—well, how can I say it?—um—possibly you're not as interesting as you could be, or well—uh—maybe boring."

Now that was a dangerous thing to say, and it wasn't a very boring evening from that point, I'll tell you that!

Naturally Jeannie was defensive and I got scared of the can of worms I had opened. I remember hearing her say that she had no problem in talking with the children, who are now adults. They enjoy talking to her. She was right, and I had to admit that she easily talked with other people and friends. Then she lowered the boom: "Maybe the person who is boring is *you*."

I didn't answer her then for she had scored a bull's-eye. What I actually had talked to Jeannie about, as I've said before, was my work and myself . . . and she listened. I was so blind and so human. I know that a person is most apt to point out the fault or weakness in the other which in reality belongs to himself. It's so easy to see other people's faults, especially when they're so familiar, so close to home. Later on that night, I mustered up some more courage and asked for more feedback about myself. "What else have you been trying to say to me that would help me grow?"

With a hesitant voice, which trembled a little, she said, "You've changed in the last ten years. I don't know how to say this, but you're not as kind a person as you were in the early years of our marriage when you were in the ministry. I don't know if it's because you're a psychologist, or if it's your success, or maybe it was a result of the three years you spent working in the drug culture, but you've become harder. Sometimes when I ask you something, there's such a flash of anger and violence in your eyes and face. I've been scared and shaky, uncertain of what I should talk to you about. When would it be safe? I guess I've come up with some dumb answers and some dumb comments because I've been so uneasy in our relationship. It's been very hard at times to know how much I could say to you."

Have We Changed Without Knowing It?

I think you call this gut-level communication, because my gut was hurt by what I was hearing. In the days that followed I was disgusted and ashamed of myself—not only for being so blind, but because I had been a kind person, and still pictured myself a kind person. It wasn't becoming a psychologist, but it was those years working in the drug culture that had changed me.

Those were hard years. A person couldn't survive by being a nice, kind do-gooder. I was in a criminal world trying to salvage sad, troubled, messed-up kids. It was a hard-core world of dope fiends, and not a very pretty world. I know some people don't like that old-fashioned term "dope fiend," but I think it's a valid description. A dope fiend is somebody who rips off his mother's color TV to pay for his habit. The mother finally settles for a used black and white TV so it won't be stolen by her son. It's a world of con artists, thieves, overdoses, and murders. I heard rumors of paranoid dealers who were talking of putting out a contract on me, because they believed I was a snitch. One day as I left the office the secretary said, "Don't go out yet, a sniper is shooting up the parking lot, waiting for you to come out." I decided I could wait for a while.

I once even had to go to the city drunk tank to confront a speed freak who wanted to kill me. He'd been picked up on a drunk charge. Someone he'd been shooting dope with warned me that he was crazy from speed, and when he was crazy, he loved to shoot guns. He was paranoid about me, so I was to be his target. I confronted him and I said, "Hey, punk, don't ever let me hear you saying that you are going to kill me. I'm no snitch. I'm so blankety-blank mad at you that I could almost lose my nonviolent commitment and beat your head in. If I ever hear of you wanting to kill me again, I'll get real angry and do that first." He denied that it was he. Then I told him his mother had warned me, and that a girl in the county hospital came out of her psychosis to warn me. When I left the jail, I wished him a Merry Christmas.

The confrontation game of therapy in gutter language and screaming at someone on the hot seat was brutal therapy. It was a hardening experience. Then in the staff games, when it's your turn to be on the hot seat, the intensity is the same. I didn't sound like a preacher man, but a gutter man using foul, four-letter words. I knew too much about organized drug smuggling. It was a strange, strange world I lived in, and I hardened in the process. Now I'm working on my goal to be a kind man again. What I experienced became a part of me, but I'm working at shedding the effects.

A strange picture of myself just flashed across the inner eye of my mind. It showed a very violent, people-loving, humorous, solitary, private family man. That's me. I recognize I need my private solitary times. That's a valid part of me. I have so much more to learn about so many different things. I cherish my time alone to read, to think, and to write. Even some of my relaxation is solitary. I play around with a trumpet and tenor sax, which I play just for me. I play not to be a performer, but to lose myself in music for a while. Maybe thirty minutes a day is mine. I'm accepting this as a part of me, and yet I also accept the responsibility to take the time and the commitment to grow in communication with my wife.

Why Is It So Hard to Talk?

Could it be that I just got in a lazy rut and developed a bad habit? If I'm in a rut, then it's my rut, and I have the responsibility to get out of it with no excuses.

The major communication problem between a man and a woman is poor listening skills due to sexual differences in male-female communication. In seminars I give some simple listening exercises. The first one requires that a person send a message to another person, and the receiver can only use nonverbal gestures of listening. With the discussion following the exercise, the listeners report consistently that it's hard to just listen to a person, because you're soon thinking of your responses and you want to come back at the communicator as soon as possible. Once you begin to think, your ability to listen decreases.

The next exercise is a very simple one. The hardest part of this one is for the participants to listen to the instructions. A person is instructed to repeat exactly what another person said to them in a short sentence, and then the other person can agree or not agree.

It is an interesting experience when a person doesn't have to make a judgment, criticize, or evaluate a message being sent, or have to think of an answer. He tries only to capture the other person's feelings and where he is "coming from."

People in these exercises experience a real change. They are hearing not words but a person, perhaps for the first time.

The Two Levels of Communication

The sexual bias in communication is a reality. There is a difference between how a man and a woman listen and communicate, and this is one of the major reasons why it's so hard to talk and be effective in communication. Human communication is a two-level process. The first level is concerned with the objective, logical, content aspect of a message or a report . . . the problem-solving aspect.

The second level of a message emphasizes the subjective side of that message . . . how it affects the relationship. It has a command aspect: what is to be done with the content of the message. It also says something about who's in charge of the relationship.

To put it simply, the first level is content and objectivity, the second level is always about relationships and is subjective. Men are more comfortable and communicate more frequently on the first level. Women are more tuned in to how the content will affect a relationship, and what effect the message will have for them on a subjective basis.

For the sake of illustration: The husband comes home from work and as he walks into the kitchen his wife says, "There's the garbage." The husband agrees with her, "Yes, there's the garbage." He goes on and fixes himself a drink and wonders, "Gee, I wonder if the little woman is cracking up? She needed me to reassure her that that was garbage." Meanwhile, back in the kitchen, the wife is either coming to a fast boil or preparing a lengthy sulk: "He doesn't care about me anymore. He knows what I wanted him to do, take out the garbage. He's so selfish. I want help around the house. That's what a man is for, but he doesn't want to help."

That night when they go to bed, the husband is aware that

the wife has been sulking all evening; she's not in the mood for love and, in fact, is quite frigid in the bedroom. So with his keen, analytical mind he asks his wife, "Honey, what's the matter with you?"

To which she replies, "You know very well what's the matter with me."

"No, I don't, honey, really I don't," says the husband.

"Well, it's—never mind—you wouldn't understand it yourself," she snaps.

"Well, give me a chance please."

"Okay, Buster, you asked for it. If all you want from me is to be a maid, a cook, and a mistress, go ahead."

"But I still don't understand," says the husband.

"How dense can you be? When you came home I said there's the garbage, and all you did was agree with me. You knew I wanted you to take the garbage out. But no, you just said, 'Yes, there's the garbage,' and went on and fixed yourself a drink."

"Well, confound it, woman, if you wanted me to take out the garbage why didn't you just come out and say it directly? 'Please take out the garbage,' and I would have taken out the garbage. That garbage has been stinkin' up our marriage all night."

Sound familiar? The husband, with his first-level bias for content, heard just the report about the garbage, not the request on the relationship level from his wife, who was asking, "Please, will you take out the garbage?" The man wants the direct problem-solving logical communciation, but his wife is programmed to be nondirective, nonaggressive, to be helpless and use emotional ploys. The wife assumes that if he loved her he would hear that she was asking him in a nondirect way to do her a favor.

When offering a woman some advice or disagreeing with a woman's statement, many a man has been bewildered to see her hurt or angered because of over-personalizing what he said. Men can usually discuss different points of view with each other without feeling personally attacked by any disagreement. I know this is a generalization only.

When I used to come home from the shrink shop, I would often be emotionally drained, so I would tell Jeannie, "Don't ask me what's new. Please, give me ten minutes to get my head together, and most importantly, please don't personalize my silence. It has nothing to do with our relationship."

Men are trained to be more logical, to use deductive reasoning, and to use facts to express their ideas and prove their points. Woman are more attuned to the subjective side of a message. They use nondirective mannerisms and maneuvers, because they have not been programmed to be assertive. Women have also been rumored to use guilt: "If you really loved me . . .!" Every once in a while women use tantrums and tears to achieve a goal in communication. I've often been amazed at the elaborate schemes and ploys a woman will devise to manipulate a man to get her way, hoping for the ultimate achievement: that he will think it was his idea.

Direct and Indirect Communication

What is a way out of this communication mess between the sexes? If I knew the answer I would be a rich man. I know there will be more effective dialogue between men and women when men can listen and respond to the second level of communication and become more sensitive and aware that it's not only what is said that is important in a dialogue, but how it will affect the relationship and how it will be received on the subjective side. When women learn that they can give themselves permission to abandon their helpless programming, emotional poise, deviousness, and manipulation and just be more direct in expressing what they're thinking and feeling, I think they'll also have more understanding.

I realize that women are frightened by the fear of being

labeled aggressive, pushy, castrating, or hostile if they become more direct, but they can be more direct in communication while still being gentle and tender. Men can learn how to be more gentle and tender in their communication and more empathetic. As a man, I'm not threatened nor do I feel a woman is less than I if she can simply report on what she feels and needs. It would simplify communication so much, and I would be eternally grateful; then it wouldn't be so hard to talk.

There are a couple of instances that may help wives understand why at times a man is silent. First, if a man has some major problems and decisions involving his career, he may withdraw mentally as he is turning them over in his mind. Now, his silence and withdrawal can bug a woman. It has been noticed that some women will persist in making inquiries about what is on their husband's mind. (Wasn't that a beautiful way of not saying a wife has been nagging her husband?) Finally the husband shares with his wife that he is very worried about being fired, or losing the business, or being sued, or whatever it is that's of major consequence, and the wife panics and screams and says, "I don't want to hear about *that.*" *That* news is threatening to her basic security.

I have used this technique with Jeannie: "I will tell you what's on my mind if you promise not to freak out, or faint, or give me an answer. I would like to use you as a sounding board to help clarify my own thinking." Believe me, sometimes we need to realize that God gave us *two* ears and *one* mouth for a reason.

There's another reason why a man may find it difficult to talk to his wife. He believes that he is so much more superior, intelligent, and worldly-wise than his wife . . . that his is such a big world and her world is such a little world. His masculine ego doesn't allow him to come down to talk to this second-class citizen called his wife. After all, what does she know? A man will never find out unless he's willing to shut up and listen to his wife. For in truth the woman of today is very well educated, probably more widely read and aware of what's happening in the world than her husband. Maybe a man uses his superiority trip as a means of controlling the relationship with his wife, and he's afraid to find out how wise she is. This is a stupid reason, because honestly, if people are to grow and love in any relationship, then there must be a freedom to speak openly, to speak the truth lovingly, and be free with one another.

Thomas Hora once said, "To understand himself, man needs to be understood by another, to be understood by another, he needs to understand the other."

CHECKPOINT

1. What subjects are easy for you to discuss with your wife? What subjects are more difficult?

2. Are you a good listener? Why or why not?

3. Does your wife communicate in a different way than you do?

4. What makes you withdraw rather than communicate?

—12—

PASSION
AND THE
DECISION
TO LOVE

What is love? I don't know of any topic surrounded by more confusion. People fall in love, get married, live together, fall out of love, get divorced, and possibly fall in love again, and it seems the cycle is repeated, only faster this time. "Love is never having to say you're sorry." The person who wrote that had never been in love, or surely had never been married.

As a society, we have been incurable romanticists. We fall in love and get married. I wonder if people make a mistake in thinking they're in love when maybe they are just "in heat." Sexual allure, passion, the "buzz," and sexual energy provide a strong motivation for the attraction between men and women. Love is more than just a beautiful, exciting, passionate, emotional, and physical buzz that goes off in a person. I'm not knocking sexual passion, which draws people together and is exciting and feels so good. Passion is a very important part of love, but passion alone in a relationship can be physiological infatuation without any decision to love, make a commitment, or develop the intimacy of self-disclosure and acceptance. It is like "puppy love," and the real problem with puppy love is that it leads a dog's life.

Passion has its own chemistry. It can create molecular interaction that sets off a chain reaction of hot and heavy emotions quickly, but passion alone cannot sustain its intensity or maintain that level for a long-term relationship. Life isn't fair!

A Three-Legged Stool

Love is like a three-legged stool. The three legs that hold the stool upright are passion, commitment (the decision to love), and intimacy. If the three legs are balanced, the stool is usable, but you can't sit on a one-legged stool whether the leg be passion, or commitment, or intimacy. All three are needed in marriage. I believe that one of the main reasons there is an increase in divorce in marriages of twenty-five to thirty-five years is that the couple realizes that the fires of passion in love have long burned out. They have left a boring relationship with no real intimacy, just the habit of marriage, the dual commitment to stay with each other.

In T. S. Eliot's *The Cocktail Party*, Edward, in talking to his wife, Lavinia, says "I've often wondered why you married me." Lavinia responds, "Well, you were really rather attractive, you know, and you kept on saying that you were in love with me. I believe you were trying to persuade yourself you were. I seemed always on the verge of some wonderful experience and it never happened. I wonder how you could have ever thought you were in love with me."[1]

Let's take a look at the decision to love and to make a commitment for marriage. The value of commitment to marriage has slipped rather badly in the past few decades. When Jeannie and I got married, there was a strong commitment toward marriage until death do us part. It was a decision to solve whatever problems we would have in the framework of our marriage. We did not have one foot in the door of marriage and the other foot outside of marriage so in case things didn't work out too well, we could easily leave and get a divorce.

There is a story about a married couple in their nineties who came to a judge for a divorce. The judge was stunned and perplexed. He asked them how long they had been married and the husband responded, "Seventy years."

"Have you wanted a divorce for a long time?" asked the judge.

"Oh, yes," replied the wife.

"But why did you wait so long?" asked the puzzled judge.

The couple replied, "We had to wait until our children had died."

A Lifetime Commitment

Bill Roberts, who is a sociologist on the staff at the University of Arizona's College of Medicine, and his wife, who has a graduate degree in family studies, conducted a research study of fifty couples in the Tucson area who had been married fifty years or more. The Robertses wanted to know what were the basic characteristics of these successful marriages. They found four characteristics: "The couples were both independent and interdependent; they were satisfied with themselves as individuals; they were optimistic; and they were flexible enough to roll with both the good and hard times. At the heart of all this data was the acceptance of the idea that once married, the individuals were committed to a lifetime together. For all of the couples this meant persevering through the Great Depression, a time which all listed as having been the most trying time in their marriage."[2]

In the decade of the 1980s we not only see divorce escalating, but we see a fear of commitment in young men to get married. In 1970 19 percent of the men between the ages of twenty-five and twenty-nine were unmarried; in 1986 39 percent of this age group were unmarried.[3] What are the reasons for the delay of marriage and fear of commitment by young men? Have we created such a self-centered group of men that they ask, "How can I do my own thing and still be committed to a marriage?"

I was lunching with a couple of successful dentists when one said to the other, "Isn't this the day you are going to get married?"

"Yes, it was to be my wedding date, but when I realized that if I married her, she would automatically have joint ownership of everything I own, I just could not handle that part of marriage."

In over thirty years of marriage counseling, and premarital counseling, I have never seen such a fear of commitment and so much self-centeredness.

Loving or in Love?

I wonder how many of us confuse being in love with loving a person. I have a sneaky suspicion that a number of us enter marriage carrying a bucket of love that is only half-full, hoping our marriage partner will fill up our bucket of love to the brim. But so often the other person is also carrying around half a bucket of love and hoping and expecting the other to fill it to the brim. This creates a desperate situation of disappointment and frustration. If one person is to have a full bucket of love, the other one is empty; or there is a standoff and two people are frustrated and angry. They feel cheated and unloved because their buckets of love are only half-full and neither is willing to fill the other's bucket. Love is the decision to empty yourself of love so the other can be full to overflowing. Love is like that. In order to keep it, you have to give it away.

As I listen to couples discussing their marital problems, it's easy to detect the one who has already made the decision to terminate the marriage. When that person is confronted about his or her lack of desire to work toward a reconciliation of the marital differences, the person often says, "But I don't love my spouse anymore. I don't have any feelings of love; therefore, we should get a divorce."

My response isn't popular. "Love isn't an emotion, but a decision. Once a person decides not to love another, the emotional feelings of love are gone because of the decision." Now there might be a few of you who object to my statement that love is a decision with no conditions. Does a person just flat out decide to say, "Okay, I love you?" Is it that simple?

No, it isn't. The decision to love a person involves a commitment and an investment of energy. The decision to love isn't a passive act but always involves personal activity.

Deciding to Love

When I decide to love, it means that I not only put forth the energy but that I decide to accept the other and to allow the other the awareness that this decision to love is unconditional. That's so easy to say but difficult to live out.

Most of us are not accepting of others and do not love without conditions. We might more truthfully say, "I love you because I can redo, remake, rescue, or rearrange this about you. Then, when I'm finished, you will be so lovable." The person to whom all of this redoing and remodeling is aimed may not experience this as love and, in fact, may resent the conditions set in order to experience acceptance.

Conditional acceptance leads to frustrations and friction, not love. It's so human to say, "I like this about you, but I can't accept these other qualities about you." We don't give people space to be themselves, and we add to the confusion with a secret picture of what they should be in order to be acceptable; but we fail to communicate this hidden ideal, or fantasy, to which they are always being compared. The other person experiences the frustration and anger of fighting a ghost with unknown shape and qualities.

The truth is, when we want another to change, it's as though we are saying, "I need to be loved, and if you change in these directions, then I will be loved." That isn't love, but the need to be loved.

Jeannie had experienced a very trying and emotionally upsetting day. A lack of estrogen was taking its toll on her emotional life. She had gone out to a social function with some friends, and it had been a disaster from her point of view. That night I held her in my arms while she cried and said, "I'm just falling apart. No matter how I try to keep myself together, I can't help it, and I am afraid that because of how I am and how I've been during this period in my life, you'll get tired of me and leave me." After she verbalized her deepest fear, she trembled all over.

I said to her, "Jeannie, I made a decision to love, and that is the basis of our relationship. It means that I accept all of you, as you have accepted all of me. This means that your nervousness, your depression, your irritability, and your shakiness is accepted as well as your good qualities, and this doesn't change the basic decision to love you. That doesn't change with your moods. I may react and snap back, because I am human, but our relationship is based on the decision to love, and every night when you go to sleep, I want you to know that you are loved and accepted."

Carl Rogers talks about becoming a self-actualized human being as a requirement for having healthy relationships. He says:

> All of this means that each partner is developing what I like to call an "internal locus of evaluation." By this I am saying that the value, the meaning that an experience has for you is not determined by what your partner says, or your parents

decide, or your church rules, or your school evaluates, but by the way it "feels" to you in your very deepest level of experiencing. For instance, all of the outside influences I mentioned may say that a given experience of sexual intercourse in your marriage is right, legal, and proper, and shows love. You know all this, and yet it was one person being used by another. It was a pretense, a fraud, and contained no real love. When you have an internal center of evaluation, it is a second type of judgment on which you rely, which guides your next behaviors. It also implies that you are not governed by the "shoulds" and "oughts" which all the aspects of our culture are so ready to substitute for the values you are discovering in and by yourself.[4]

The decision to love another is based on a person trusting himself, believing in himself, and being free to give and share with another so that they can grow and experience themselves as unique and loving persons.

Learning to Express Love

Love is learned behavior. A person can learn to hate; so too a person can learn to love and to give of himself in a relationship. I know this doesn't sound too romantic . . . learning how to love, like learning how to do arithmetic problems. On the other hand, it could be the most enjoyable homework a person experiences.

I've known some men who find it difficult to express their love. Recently a man in a seminar confessed that he hadn't known how important it was to communicate with his wife. He thought everything was fine until she said, "I want a divorce." That woke him up, and he began to realize that if he didn't communicate, there was no expression of love. In time, the wife was able to say, "Yes, I no longer resent being trapped, so to speak, as a wife, a mother, and by running a household, because once there was the decision to communicate and to love, all things fell into their place and their order."

One man, who confessed to having difficulty in expressing his love, said that he didn't mean that he didn't love his wife, but he found it very hard to touch her, or to get in touch with his deepest needs and allow himself to express them. "In fact, if I showed my love, I was fearful of being vulnerable again." Then he realized that for him, as when a child growing up with Mother, to show a woman that you loved her meant falling under her control. Thus he felt that to love a woman was to be controlled by a woman.

There's an old French saying, "Love is the child of freedom, never of domination." It is this fear of domination and control that bottles up many a man. However, he can learn how to say and do loving things, and to find the words to express what is deep in his heart. It helps a man to unlock his heart to begin by writing his thoughts down on a piece of paper, something like writing a love letter to his wife, but without the fear of criticism or rejection. It's like finally having permission to be free to unlock the door and let the love flow.

Recommitment

We need to decide to love and to invest ourselves in a relationship, because most of us become careless and sloppy in marriage and drift into ruts after so many years. We take each other for granted. There are also plateaus that marriages go through. The early years you hustle and work together to reach a certain goal, and then you stop for a while. And then you have another plateau. The fires of love can burn out, and a divorce can threaten simply because people haven't realized that the decision to love is not made at the altar but is made daily. Marriage is a job—a full-time job.

Those of us forty-five and older are now divorcing at a record rate. There are many reasons for the rising divorce rate but a prime one is that the decision not to stay married is more acceptable than it was. I agree that some marriages should end rather than continue on their self-destructive way. But I keep wondering how much our self-oriented, give-me-space-to-do-my-own-thing society has seduced many of us to divorce rather than to love and grow in the intimacy of marriage.

I guess what I want to say is that the decision to love means we quit playing games with each other, withholding love, or using blackmail . . . that we accept, we give, and this becomes the dynamic that creates a new energy and power. I know for myself that without love I am nothing and without my giving of love I cannot experience the greatest of all joys and that is the gift of love. There must be a gift given in order to receive, and yet love is a very selfish act because the more I love, the more I receive. In a way, love is like a boomerang—I throw it out and it comes back to me with a little bit more added to it.

In going on my pilgrimage, I've returned to some old friends like the books of Viktor Frankl. I will never forget when he was talking about that cold, bleak winter day out in the forest when he was on a work detail while in the death camp in Auschwitz. The men were reduced to just shells, skin stretched over bones, and yet they had the fire and determination not to give in to tyranny and death. Viktor Frankl began thinking of his wife, and his very bleak existence. He didn't know whether his wife was dead or alive at another camp. In truth, she was dead, but he wrote these words about what he experienced that cold, bleak day in the woods:

> A thought transfixed me, for the first time in my life I saw the truth as it is set into a song by so many poets, proclaimed

as the final wisdom by so many thinkers. The truth that love is the ultimate and highest goal to which man can aspire. Then I grasped the meaning of the greatest secret that poetry and human thought and belief have to impart. The salvation of man is through love and in love.[5]

CHECKPOINT

1. Three ingredients of love are passion, commitment, and intimacy. Can you think of other ingredients that might be added to these?

2. Why have young people developed a different attitude toward commitment than previous generations have had?

3. What is meant by "carrying into marriage a bucket that is only half-full"?

4. "Love is learned behavior." Do you agree?

5. "Love is the child of freedom, never of domination" is an old French saying. What does this mean to you? What might it mean in your marriage?

—13—
INTIMACY
IN
MARRIAGE

I have said that love is a three-legged stool made up of passion, commitment, and intimacy. Intimacy in marriage can be seen in a couple who have been married for forty to sixty years and realizing that through the years they have even come to look alike. There is such a deep emotional bonding and knowing of each other and facing all the trials, heartaches, and setbacks that life can throw at them, that there is really no new challenge or threat except death. And usually, by this time, each one has made peace with death and, if they are Christians, death "ain't no big thing" because Jesus Christ has defeated death in His resurrection, and when Jesus comes again, they too shall rise from the dead "to meet the Lord in the air and remain with him forever" (*see* Thessalonians 4:17).

In most Christian marriage ceremonies we hear these words of Jesus, "Have you not read that he who made them from the beginning made them male and female, and said, 'For this reason a man shall leave his father and mother and be joined to his wife, and the two shall become one flesh'? So they are no longer two but one flesh. What therefore God has joined together, let not man put asunder" (Matthew 19:4–6 RSV).

Two becoming one in marriage is much, much more than the intimacy of sexual relationships between a man and a woman. Christian marriage is to be a spiritual covenant: a man, a woman, and God. Intimacy is a process of opening up to each other, accepting each other as he or she is rather than how you want them to be. It is an ongoing process of sharing hopes, dreams, disappointments, heartaches, and not allowing walls to separate you through lack of forgiveness, resentment, and bitterness. Remember, those of you who have been married for a number of years, the shock that came with the realization that the person you wedded is not the person you are going to live with in marriage. Usually this realization takes place shortly after the marriage ceremony.

Robert J. Trotter writes: "The best single predictor of happiness in a relationship is not how you feel about the other person but the difference between how you would ideally like the other person to feel about you and how you think he or she actually feels about you." In other words, the first big test of a relationship is how far apart are a person's needs and expectations in the relationship and what the person is actually receiving from the other. The greater the distance between expectations, or hidden agendas, a person has in a marriage, and reality, the greater the chance for the relationship to fail or not reach the desired bonding of emotional acceptance and intimacy.[1]

A divorced woman told me about the time she was driving her car downtown with her five-year-old son, who, as they passed or were passed by a car with a man and woman in the car, would say, "Married . . . single . . . single . . . married . . . married," to each car. The mother asked her son what he was doing and he replied, "Oh, just counting the cars with married or single people in them."

She was surprised and asked him, "How can you tell if a couple in a car is married or single?"

"Oh, that's easy, Mom, the single man and woman sit real close together and the married man and woman sit far apart."

Marital Priorities

Most men do not place the marriage relationship as high on their list of priorities or values as do women. Thus the woman assumes more responsibility as she has a higher priority and value on the marriage relationship. Traditionally, the man's role has been to spend the major share of his energy in being the provider for the family. Traditionally, a woman has been programmed, especially in middle- and upper middle-class America, to find a good ambitious, strong man to provide for her and the children so she can, in a sense, play house. Somehow she belongs to her husband and she should cater to his needs, moods, and personality; and he will protect her and make the big decisions for her.

Some men actually court a woman, marry her, then treat her like a possession, much in the same way they own a house, a car, a boat, stock, or anything else. This does not make for a happy marriage, much less an intimate relationship.

Biblical Guidance

In talking about the kind of relationship there should be between a husband and wife, many preachers, male of course, love to preach on the words of the apostle Paul, who wrote, "Wives, be subject to your husbands, as to the Lord. For the husband is the head of the wife as Christ is the head of the church, his body, and is himself its Savior. As the church is subject to Christ, so let wives also be subject in everything to their husbands" (Ephesians 5:22–24 RSV).

I have counseled wives who have been viciously beaten by their husbands, and who have gone to their pastors for counseling only to be told, in effect, that somehow the beatings were their fault and they needed to be more submissive to their husband and pray more for him. Most of the time the pastor never asked the husband to come for counseling. In fact I have never heard a minister preach on the twenty-fifth verse in the fifth chapter of Ephesians which says, "Husbands, love your wives, as Christ loved the church and gave himself up for her" (RSV).

Jesus told His disciples that His role and theirs was to be different in regard to exercising authority. "Whoever would be great among you must be your servant, and whoever would be first among you must be slave of all. For the Son of man also came not to be served but to serve and to give his life as a ransom for many" (Mark 10:43–45 RSV).

About the Last Supper we read: "And how he loved his disciples! So he got up from the supper table, took off his robe, wrapped a towel around his loins, poured water into a basin, and began to wash the disciples' feet and to wipe them with the towel he had around him" (John 13:3–5).

So husband, if you are to love your wife as Christ loved the church, you must serve her instead of expecting her to serve you. You must be a servant to your wife. According to Isaiah 53, Jesus was the suffering servant. If you love your wife as Jesus loved the church, you will be willing to offer your very life for her.

I guess these words of Scripture are such painful words for husbands to hear that preachers would rather not offend the husbands in the church, giving their wives such dangerous words about the Christian relationship between husbands and wives.

I must admit that most of us men do tend to feel we are superior to women. A woman is to be dependent on the man and submissive to his wishes when decisions are to be made. But this definition of a relationship only works when a husband has married a very dependent, doormat type of woman. Look out if that woman decides to be a person and not be a weak, dependent doormat. The revolution in the relationship will most likely end in divorce unless the couple goes into marriage counseling to work out a new definition of their relationship with a whole new set of ground rules.

Dependence and Independence

The women's movement has had a very positive effect in helping women realize their personhood as first-class citizens. It has given women much more self-esteem, self-confidence, and independence from an unhealthy dependency. This change is a challenging one for marriage and intimacy.

In some women there are two strong needs which compete for supremacy. One is the need to be the dominant one in a relationship, and the other need is to remain dependent on, or submissive to her husband. A strong need of self-expression and independence in a woman can create serious problems. It seems that if a woman becomes dominant in a relationship, she often loses her man or he becomes less a person she can respect. How do we find the healthy balance in this drive toward personhood and independence and still recognize that in a healthy marriage relationship there is both independence and interdependence? We must realize that neither party in a marriage owns the other, nor should it be anyone's purpose in a relationship to live at another's expense, nor is one's spouse solely responsible for one's happiness.

Time Together

One of the most difficult barriers to intimacy in marriages today, with both spouses working, is to find time to spend together. This is especially true for the successful career woman whom I often hear in therapy sounding a lot like many complaining husbands: that her husband doesn't understand or appreciate how hard she has to work even when she spends long hours on the job. Remember the song "A Time For Us"?

Well, too often the time is very short and both spouses are very exhausted. In fact, too exhausted to enjoy the "good life" their combined incomes produce.

Robert J. Steinberg and Sandra Wright conducted research on why so many relationships fail. Some of their findings are not very encouraging. The ability to make love, for example, often goes just at the time when it is becoming more important. The ability to communicate, physical attractiveness, having good times, sharing interests, the ability to listen, respect for each other, romantic love—they all declined. In fact, Steinberg says, almost every factor except mutual religious beliefs decreased over time.

Expressing Love

One of the most moving scenes in the musical *Fiddler on the Roof* is when the husband sings to the wife, "Do you love me?" His wife, working in the kitchen, is very surprised by her husband's question and replies, "I married you."

"But, do you love me?"

The wife responds to his persistent question by reciting how she cooks for him, cleans the house, has children by him, but the husband isn't hearing the answer he needs to hear: "Yes, I love you."

For marriages to last and not just endure, love must be expressed in words and loving actions, throughout the years of marriage. When the children have left home and there is an empty-nest syndrome, too often a couple realizes how they have drifted apart. Picture the husband who takes his wife out to dinner and when he isn't talking about his work and his wife isn't talking about their children, a strange hush falls across the dinner table, almost as though they were strangers. This can be a dangerous time in a marriage or a real opportunity for a couple to recommit their love for each other.

The Empty Nest

A pastor friend of mine was talking about the empty nest at his home since the children were all grown and on their own. He said: "This empty nest is really great. I love it. I just hope and pray that the kids don't come home again to live. My wife and I love being just the two of us."

For the Olsons, after thirty-five years of marriage, it's just the two of us rambling about in a big house. We recognize that this is a time of danger and a time of opportunity. We feel we must set new goals in our relationship and for the years ahead. I realize that I have been a bit jealous of the close relationship between Jeannie and our daughter Jan. It has made me feel alone and left out at times. I realize that now that Jan is married, Jeannie and I will have the opportunity to build a closer relationship for the two of us. It is time to clean off the barnacles of bad habits we have acquired in the past thirty-five years. We need to invest in each other with a renewed conscious effort and commitment. I believe it's well worth the effort to put that energy into the relationship. There are so many new vistas to be discovered and places to see but, more important, there's the realization that in our marriage we must not settle down in a boring rut—two aging, lonely people living out separate lives under one roof called a home. The challenge is to grow both as individuals as well as a couple.

Our Deepest Needs

What does a man want, or need from his relationship with his wife? I can't answer that question. Each man must search for his own answer. I know that I'm a hugger and a toucher, and I have a whole bunch of love to give to my wife, children, and other people. I also know that my deepest need is to be loved by a woman. That love is the bridge that spans the gulf of my aloneness. It's the key that unlocks the door of my private, lonely prison. I don't know why it's so hard for us men to admit that what we want most of all is to be loved by a woman. This means far more than just being supplied with a sex partner. It means being needed, valued, cared for, trusted, appreciated, admired—yes, even knowing your wife is proud of you.

A few years ago I came straight out and told Jeannie, "I need your love, and I want you to show your love by words, touching, caressing, and hugging." I asked for a physical communication from her, and she responded.

Recently, however, I sometimes wonder what's the matter with me, because I've been fussy with her, even curt at times. I've said, "There's no reason and no excuse for my behavior." Finally I realized that I needed to say, "I want you to let me know that I'm attractive to you, that you still think of me as somebody sexually attractive, that you still dig me, that just because we've been married for a number of years, we don't stop communicating that way." So I quit dumping on her and said, "Hey, this is what I need." Then I was able to communicate and the problem was solved.

Also, as a man who works hard, carries a lot of responsibilities, and supports and provides for his family, I need to be told, "Thanks for working so hard for us." I know other men feel that way because when wives have said, "Hey, honey, thanks for all the effort and energies put out to provide for our family," they are startled to see how overwhelmed and thankful their husbands are that they are appreciated and not taken for granted. Of course, the same works in reverse.

My wife is very important to me. Her belief and trust in me have been incredible. She has given me the freedom to be me, to change careers and to upset the economic stability of our home life. There have been years in our marriage when we weren't poor, we just didn't have any money, but she never complained. I wonder if Jeannie does believe me when I say, "I need your approval and appreciation." That's still very vital to me. Please hear me clearly, it's not a mother's approval and appreciation, but the woman who's my wife.

I once saw a television show that was beautifully touching and realistic. It was the story of a detective whose wife was pleading with him to be home in time for dinner because they were having company. He promises that this time he will be home on time, but crime doesn't take place only between nine and five. Thus, you see this detective chasing the criminal down the beach late at night, and you know that he is not only in trouble with the criminal, but he's going to be in trouble with the hostess at home. Finally he wrestles the man down in the surf and arrests him.

The next scene is that of soggy shoes and wet trousers slowly walking up the steps from the garage, suggestive of a man's last walk to the gallows. He knows he's very late. He expects the wrath of his woman to befall him the moment he steps into the kitchen. So it is with bowed head that he opens the door and is greeted by his lovely, charming wife. In a state of shock, as he starts to apologize, he hears these words, "Honey, I called the other couple. I said they would have to take a rain check on dinner tonight since you were out on a case and would most likely be late." Then she really bowls him over when she says, "Honey, I've taken you for granted and have been only thinking of myself and of my own convenience. I've forgotten that you have been out working hard for the family, risking your life, not only for our family but for our community." Then he sees the table set for two with candles and wine, and he asks, "Can dinner wait a few minutes?" She smiles and says, "Yes." And arms wrapped around each other they walk up to the bedroom, and as they put their hand on the bedroom doorknob, there is a cry of a baby in the next room. That was one of the most loving and realistic shows I've seen in many a year.

Not by Human Effort Alone

I am convinced that a love that continally seeks to move toward a deeper intimacy in marriage, where a couple is comfortable just being together, being best friends, being kind to each other, and forgiving each other, is not very easily achieved by human effort alone. It takes a spiritual bonding in God's love and in His presence in the marriage for this to happen. The greatest gift of the Holy Spirit is the gift of God's love. The apostle Paul writes about this gift of love with these words, "Love is very patient and kind, never jealous or envious, never boastful or proud, never haughty or selfish or rude. Love does not demand its own way. It is not irritable or touchy. It does not hold grudges and will hardly even notice when others do it wrong. It is never glad about injustice, but rejoices whenever truth wins out. If you love someone you will be loyal to him no matter what the cost. You will always believe in him, always expect the best of him, and always stand your ground in defending him" (1 Corinthians 13:4–7).

"There are three things that remain—faith, hope, and love—and the greatest of these is love" (1 Corinthians 13:13).

CHECKPOINT

1. Robert J. Trotter writes, "The best single predictor of happiness in a relationship is not how you feel about the other person but the difference between how you would ideally like the other person to feel about you and how you think he or she actually feels about you." What does that mean?

2. What are the implications of Paul's command, "Husbands, love your wives as Christ loved the church"?

3. What problems are faced when a wife works outside the home? Are there other problems when a wife doesn't work outside the home?

4. What are the challenges of the "empty nest"?

5. Do you praise your wife for how she looks, what she does, and what she is?

—14—

THE
HEALING
OF
RELATIONSHIPS

After another bad fight the night before and sleeping in separate rooms, Jane speaks to husband Ron at breakfast. "Honey, our marriage is in serious trouble and I don't want a divorce. Let's go to a professional marriage counselor for help."

"A marriage counselor," snorts Ron, "That won't help our marriage, but it might do you some good so why don't you make an appointment."

Men are so afraid to seek help in counseling. Too many men would rather fail at their marriage than admit that something is wrong and that they should seek help. There is a feeling of failure and even shame for a man to seek help. I will never forget a young man who sat in a chair in my office with his eyes closed, head hanging down, because he was a "macho policeman" who felt he should be able to handle his problems in marriage without any outside help. Men have principles about things like this—the "stupid-stubborn-pride principle."

I have been successful in having both partners participate in marriage counseling because I stress that it is a joint venture to solve the marriage problems. As I said earlier, I have a simple rule that no one speaks for the other person—each person, after all, views the marriage from his own unique perspective. If a husband is reluctant to come for marriage counseling, I call him and ask him if he wants his wife to speak for him in the counseling. Usually the husband does not like the idea of his wife speaking for him, so he comes.

I have a fantasy about a couple coming in for marriage counseling. I ask the couple what the problems are in the relationship. The husband replies, "Ken, it's all my fault. I have taken my wife for granted all these years. I don't do the little things in marriage that would mean so much to her. I'm so preoccupied with my job and my interests that frankly I ignore her by being so busy. When she is starved for communication, I withdraw in silence into a television program. Then I get mad at her when we go to bed because she is not turned on sexually when I turn off the bedroom light. It's all my fault."

The wife looks at me and says, "Ken, my husband is not the problem; I am the problem in our marriage. I never thank him for working so hard for me and the children. I am never satisfied; I always want more; so I nag at him unmercifully. Is it any wonder he withdraws in silence. When I first met him, I discovered everything that he was interested in: football, basketball, hunting, western movies, ancient history. I sure fooled him because he thought I shared those interests with him. Well, I lied. I pretended to be interested in all those things until we got married. Then he found out I had suddenly lost interest in those things which were important to him. I use sex as a weapon to punish him and to get my way. No, Ken, it's all my fault."

If that ever happened, I would react by fainting from the shock of it all.

Accepting Responsibility

Instead of blaming the other and excusing his or her bad behavior as just a reaction, each person must accept his or her own responsibility in the relationship. Husband and wife are both right and both wrong, because in relationships it takes two to tangle.

For example, let's take a look at the complaint of the wife that her husband won't talk to her, and the complaint of the husband that his wife is a nag. The wife will excuse her nagging because she is just reacting to his silent behavior. "So what else could I do?" the wife asks. The husband says to the wife, "There you go again, getting it all wrong. I won't talk because you are always on my back nagging me about this or that. Naturally I don't want to talk to you." Each spouse reports what the other does that makes him or her unhappy and refuses to take responsibility for his or her own reaction, failing to see how such a response determines future behavior. It can be a relationship war without end. I won't talk because you nag. I nag because you won't talk, and on, and on.

After a few years of difficulties in solving relationship problems, a marriage often develops a negative perceptual basis. Each person expects and looks for negative behavior in the other. Negative behavior is so powerful, but when you ask a couple if they enjoy the war and being miserable, they look surprised and respond by saying they hate it. I reassure them that they have a right to be miserable since they are spending so much energy in being miserable. If the couple agrees to end the war and develop a different basis for the relationship on a more positive basis, I give them this simple homework assignment. For the following week each person is to keep track of everything the other does that is pleasing and write it down to share it at the next appointment. If a couple's relationship is based on a negative mind-set and expectation, this assignment causes them to shift their perceptions, to anticipate a positive, caring basis for the relationship. It also causes each spouse to consciously choose to act toward the other in a caring, loving way.

I will never forget Bill and June, who had been married for thirty years, but were locked into a never-ending, petty war. At the appointment when they were to report on their homework, June pulled out her list of things that Bill had done to please her the past week. As she read the list, tears of joy began to fall from his eyes. When she finished reading the list, she caught herself, and said defensively, "Well, I don't suppose you wrote a list of things I did that were pleasing to you?" Bill smiled and reached into his pocket and pulled out his list of things that June had done that pleased him in the last week. This began a whole new way of relating to each other because each was doing caring, loving things for the other.

A healthy relationship is one in which each partner tries to meet the other person's needs but never at their own expense. Once I get couples to realize that in *giving to* a relationship, the outcome is love instead of war, and they try it, they will like it. I always stress that *giving to* a relationship is not the same as *giving in to* the other. I have discovered that when I ask a person to *give* to a relationship, that often the subconscious mind adds the "in," thinking, "Here I go again *giving in to* you." I explain that the person who *gives to* a relationship so the outcome is love and not war is coming from a position of power. Anyone can go to war, but there are so few peacemakers in the world. That is why Jesus said, "Blessed are the peacemakers."

Avoiding Alienation

Peace *keeping*, on the other hand, often is only avoidance of conflicts in a relationship that cry out to be resolved. Yet how many of us are taught, "Don't make waves," "Keep the peace—at all costs," or the old chestnut, "Talk is silver, but silence is golden." A divorced mother was sharing with me that her six-year-old son came home from school and told her that his best friend, Tony, was very upset because his mom and dad fought all the time and were now getting a divorce. She said to her son, "Well, at least Daddy and I didn't fight all the time." "No, Mom," her son replied, "you and Dad never could communicate."

The opposite of love is not hate, but apathy. Learning how to fight, express anger, and hurts in ways that lead to problem solving is healing and healthy for a relationship. I wonder how many couples continue to live together physically and legally, yet are emotionally divorced with no intimacy in the relationship. Apathy and boredom create a climate conducive to affairs and a keep-the-marriage-together-for-the-sake-of-the-children attitude. The husband and wife don't fight because they can't communicate honestly and openly.

Married couples need to learn how to fight constructively and not destructively. In any marriage with a few years behind it, there will be hurts, frustrations, unmet needs, and repressed anger that may have already turned into resentment, bitterness, and hate. The repressed anger and bitterness become a wall that blocks the impulse to give love to the other. If the emotional abscesses are drained, the wall of alienation comes down and love can now be expressed and received.

Resolving Conflict

Here are some guidelines on conflict resolution.

1. Handle conflict as soon as possible.
2. Speak the truth in love and not as a weapon to hurt. Employ what I call the "Lincoln principle." "Tell the truth and you won't have so much to remember." Many people

have a hard time in letting the other know what is really hurting or bothering them.

3. Stay in the here and now. Don't bring up the garbage of the past. Remember: Love is the decision to forgive and not keep score.

4. Try to take turns in listening, and before you respond, report what you heard the other say. It is called feedback. Too many couples fight a dialogue of the deaf. No one is really listening.

5. Agree before you have a fight to call the other on what I call fouls: Name calling, and words that are spoken to *hurt*. Those are fouls. Acting as though you can read your spouse's mind is a foul. "Drunk talk" is a foul. Physical violence or very destructive talks are most likely to occur when a spouse is drunk.

6. Never try to solve a problem or meet the other's needs and frustrations during the "arsenic hour." The arsenic hour is the time of day when people in a family come home, filled with frustrations of the day, affected by the crush of traffic and low blood sugar, and needing to feel restored and cared for. The arsenic hour is the time before dinner when most family fights begin. Never give a person in the family a problem to solve or a need to be met before dinner, unless you want a war. Wait until after dinner when the need for food has been met and the blood sugar level elevated before discussion of personal problems and needs.

7. Practice problem solving without going to war. For example, when there is a conflict to be resolved, use these words, "Let's explore the problem and find solutions without exploding." Search for at least three solutions. This offers an alternative to my good solution and your stupid one.

8. Agree to end the problem solving by forgiving and hugging each other. Remember, "A hug a day keeps the shrink away."

There are times when I will meet with one partner at a time for counseling. It helps to have the person talk to me without the pressure of the other one listening, and often I will choose the stronger one in the marriage to give some suggestions for ending a particular relationship war or to change the habitual expectations of the other. Often one partner in the marriage realizes the need for therapy for the woundedness the other partner brought to the marriage. It doesn't take too long to realize when a hurting person is displacing his or her anger or fears from childhood onto the spouse.

The Power of Forgiveness

The most powerful force in the healing of wounded people is forgiveness. Forgiveness is easy to say, but in reality it is difficult to accomplish. How often you hear a person say, "I'll forgive so and so, but I'll never forget." That is not forgiveness; in fact it is an inner vow to block forgiveness by never forgetting. Inner vows are very powerful and often destructive barriers to healing. Inner vows like "I'll never love that much again," or "I'll never trust anyone again," or "I'll never forget how much you hurt me." Just check yourself to see if you have made an inner vow after being hurt in your life.

This is my definition of forgiveness: Forgiveness is the single most selfish thing I can do for myself. When I forgive someone who hurt me, who gets rid of the pain? I do. My forgiving that person does not change what happened to hurt me. It does change my reaction to the hurt. Forgiveness does not necessarily change the other person because it changes me. If there is an ongoing relationship, the change in me will often change the relationship and eventually how the other person feels about me. Forgiveness is not just an emotional feeling. It starts with the conscious decision to forgive the person who hurt me. This decision is not just made once, but each time that hurt surfaces until the pain is gone and memory fades away. Jesus was very big on forgiveness. In the Lord's prayer Jesus taught His disciples to pray, "forgive us our sins as we forgive those who sin against us." Jesus also taught,

"Listen to me! You can pray for anything, and if you believe, you have it. It's yours. (Doesn't that sound great!) But when you are praying, first forgive anyone you are holding a grudge against, so that your Father in heaven will forgive you your sins too."

Has your marriage become a grudge match that is guaranteed to destroy any passion, commitment or intimacy by the building of walls that separate you? Do you look for ways to retaliate? Marriages can become a relationship of the "dumper" and the "dumpee." Dumpers get rid of the anger and frustration by dumping it on the spouse, who becomes the "dumpee." The dumpee soon becomes the "doormat" of the marriage. Dumpees accept the emotional garbage from the dumper and hold on to it and keep it and store it forever. How do you know if you are a dumpee? Well, if you can remember the hour, the day, the year when someone hurt you, what song was playing, what clothes the other was wearing, and so on, then you are the dumpee who reigns over the garbage heap. Now if you like living in garbage, that is your right. Just don't complain that life smells, when you are sitting on top of a garbage dump. If you want to get rid of the garbage, bury it, and do not keep digging around to see if it's still there. Also instruct the dumper that you are out of the garbage business and you refuse to be dumped on again.

The apostle Paul writes, "Watch out that no bitterness takes root among you, for as it springs up it causes deep trouble, hurting many in their spiritual lives" (Hebrews 12:15). When I am hurt, I react most often with anger. If the anger is discharged verbally or through forgiveness, the energy of the anger is dissipated. Our reactions to being hurt involve a personal decision and personal responsibility for our reactions. This is seldom realized or accepted—that our reactions to being hurt are our own decisions and responsibility. Normally, when we are hurt, we feel justified for our reaction to the hurt, as though nothing else could be done but to strike back or brood about it.

The Roots of Bitterness

If you are hurt and the anger turns inward, it becomes depression, resentment, then bitterness, and finally, hate. Hate is the means by which you destroy yourself because of the actions of others. Not only is emotional health destroyed, but resentments and the roots of bitterness and hate can also make you physically ill as well as spiritually dis-eased. Jesus calls these decisions and reactions of resentment, bitterness, and hate—sin. Sin that must be confessed for God's forgiveness. Forgiveness of the person who hurt you so God will forgive you.

A man who had been married for over fifty years, but who had just recently separated from his wife, came to me for counseling. He was very upset that after all those years of marriage, he couldn't continue being married to his wife unless there was a miracle. He admitted freely that most of the problems in the marriage were his fault. "I was an alcoholic for the first eighteen years of our marriage and I was a terrible husband when I was drunk; I verbally and physically abused my wife. I don't know why she put up with it so long. I quit drinking and I have asked my wife for forgiveness and I have tried to make it up to her the rest of our married years. But I can't take any more cruel, abusive remarks from her. It's as if she can't stop trying to pay me back, so I finally had to move out."

I saw the wife at the next appointment and she said, "I'm so miserable and it's my fault. I can't control my cruel tongue. I try not to attack my husband, but no matter how hard I try, it doesn't do any good."

I asked, "Did you ever make a vow to yourself that you would never let your husband forget how much he hurt you when he was drunk?"

"Well, I guess I did make a vow like that," she replied.

"That inner vow you made will not allow your mind to release the painful memories, and it has caused you to become filled with the roots of bitterness and all the anger and bitterness are always at the surface of your conscious mind, ready to spill out the poison when you talk to your husband. To be healed you must renounce that inner vow and confess to God your sins of resentment, bitterness and hate, and ask for His forgiveness."

I next asked what other hurts in her life needed healing and she told of very painful memories of being raped when she was thirteen, resulting in the birth of a child which she gave up for adoption. The man who raped her was arrested and she had to testify against him at his trial. He swore to kill her when he got out of prison. She was raised in a small town, so everyone knew what happened to her. Instead of rallying to her support, they withdrew from her and treated her like dirt. Even her friends at school would have nothing to do with her. Tears began to flow from her eyes as those painful memories were recalled.

I then explained that I would like to pray for Jesus and the Holy Spirit to heal the painful hurts in her memory. I said, "I know you were raised in the Lutheran church and the laying on of hands for the healing of painful memories is something completely new to you. You have a right to reject my offer of prayer, because I would not want to force this on you."

She replied, "Ken, I'm desperate for help. I will try anything that will heal my hurts."

I have found that pain is the most powerful motivation for change in people's lives. When the pain becomes intolerable people will make significant changes in their lives to stop hurting so much.

I anointed her forehead with oil, and she renounced her vow and confessed the sin of making the vow, and her sins of resentment, bitterness, and hate. I took authority over her vow, and in the name of Jesus declared it broken. I asked her to forgive the man who raped her, the people who rejected her, and her husband. After that, I pronounced the absolution for her sins. I then prayed for the Holy Spirit to come and heal her. (I have learned that if I am to pray for healing for a person, I must first pray for the Holy Spirit to come with the power of healing.) I then asked Jesus to heal all the hurts of her being raped and rejected, and to heal all the painful memories of verbal and physical abuse by her husband. I then just prayed in the Spirit quietly to myself. I never know what will happen when I pray, because my responsibility is to pray and it is up to Jesus and the Holy Spirit to do the healing.

As I prayed, I experienced a powerful anointing of the Holy Spirit and the peace of God came to her. When I finished, she sat there with a peaceful smile, and thanked me. She said nothing of what she experienced, but made an appointment for the next week.

At the next appointment, she excitedly told of her miracle of healing. "Jesus came to me and healed all the painful memories in my life because I renounced the vow that I would never let my husband forget how much he had hurt me, and confessed and asked forgiveness for my sins of resentment, bitterness, and hate. Then when I forgave all the people who had hurt me, Jesus took away all that resentment, bitterness, and hate. It's a miracle. I knew it last week, but I wanted to see if it would last. I even watched a movie on television about a rape and it did not bring up all my painful memories."

It was a time of wonder and thanksgiving to God for His mercy and healing. The next week she and her husband came in together and confessed their sins against each other and forgave each other. We celebrated this powerful healing with Holy Communion, and I laid my hands on both their heads to receive God's blessing on their marriage. Needless to say, they did not need any more counseling.

Seasons of Crisis

During the seasons of crisis in a marriage, there is a danger of one of the spouses having an extramarital affair. Most likely it is the man who has the affair, but the incidence of wives having affairs has increased as women at work feel more economically secure and have more contact with men. There are some men who are habitual women chasers and go from one affair to another. At the other extreme is the man who has been married for twenty or thirty years and has never been unfaithful to his wife. The subtle erosion over time, the sameness, the boredom in the relationship, have prepared this man to be vulnerable to an affair. He knows that his marriage isn't the most exciting and their sex life has become an infrequent, passionless experience, but he hangs in there. Then he meets another woman and is shocked by the "buzz" he feels. Before he knows it, he is involved with her. If this exciting relationship continues, he may surprise his wife, family, and friends by suddenly announcing that he is getting a divorce.

The changes in her husband's behavior haven't gone unnoticed by his wife. She is deeply hurt and anguished. How could this have happened to her? He was the last person she would ever have expected to have an affair. The hurt and devastated wife can strike out in vengeance and in vindictiveness. This response will drive her husband to the other woman and the divorce court. If the wife decides to fight for her man and their marriage, she can usually achieve a successful healing of the relationship. It begins with the decision to love again and not let the roots of bitterness destroy her.

First, the wife will need to do an inventory on herself as to what part she played in the dying relationship. What changes can she make in herself and in the relationship to win her husband back? I admit that at this point most wives aren't feeling that they need to change, rather that they have been victimized, but if they want to win back their man, this is where they must start, because this kind of man usually can be won back to the marriage.

It will help a woman in this situation to write out her rage in a private journal. She should not make a morbid attempt to find out what kind of woman this "other woman" is—what kind of "low life" she is. To try to discover what the "other woman" has that she doesn't have will drive her husband further away. If she verbally runs down the other woman, tries to belittle her, she is also running down her husband who chose to have an affair with her.

Reconciliation

At this point a wife and husband need professional counseling to work out their frustrations and hurts and to achieve reconciliation in the context and safety of therapy. If the wife talks to all her friends, she will receive confusing, and usually bad, advice.

It has been my experience in over thirty years of marriage counseling, that men are far more likely to renegotiate their marriage after being involved in an affair than are women. I think that in all these years of counseling I have seen three, maybe four wives return to their husbands after becoming involved with another man. I don't know how to account for this, except that maybe by the time a married woman gets involved with another man, she has already made the decision not to love and to end the marriage. It was just a matter of time until she found someone else.

Now if the man has been deeply involved emotionally with another woman, but decides to recapture his marriage and save it, it will be a long road back, filled with ambivalent feelings, hard knocks, low points, and a few good times. The decision to love his wife again doesn't mean he can automatically turn off his thoughts, feelings, and desires for the other woman. To be so close to the decision to end the marriage and then decide to rebuild it doesn't produce an overnight miracle.

If the husband is quiet and distant at times, the wife should not make the mistake of asking him, "Are you thinking of her?" Most likely he *is* thinking of her, and if he isn't, he will start thinking of her because of the wife's suggestion. At times the husband will surely be thinking of the other woman, so don't bring it up. It only causes more hurt. Perhaps there will be times when the husband will need to communicate with the other woman, as he is working through the ending of this relationship. It is a confusing time for a man to realize he can be in love with two women at the same time. The wife must learn the painfully difficult lesson of patience. Time will provide healing for the deep hurts and devastating blows to her self-esteem.

One wife shared with me her strategy to win back her husband. "I just hung in there and mustered up the courage to be more appealing and attractive to my husband and not live with self-pity and bitterness, because I didn't want to lose him. It was funny how old sexual hang-ups disappeared when I decided to love my man."

Love is the decision to accept the reality of the unfaithfulness, forgive the spouse, and then to build a bridge of new trust on a foundation of faith, hope, and love. These words are easy to say until a person has to put them into effect. This decision to forgive and love again is very expensive, but, after all, who said that love is cheap, or who would even want cheap love?

Have an Affair—With Your Spouse

If affairs are exciting, invigorating, and stimulating, why not have an affair with your wife or your husband! I decided to have an affair with my wife. I'm a very sentimental, romantic person, even more so than Jeannie. I find myself wistfully looking at those very romantic cards which show a young couple walking hand in hand at sunset on the beach. As I read the beautiful, tender, loving words, I think, *Oh, wouldn't it be great to be young and in love again. To be starry-eyed and dreamy again.* So I decided that maybe love is wasted on the young. I started buying those cards for Jeannie, mailing them to her or putting one on her pillow so she could see it the first thing in the morning. One time when I was going to be gone for a month on a book-promotion tour, I bought nine of the most romantic cards I could find. With each card I wrote a poem and mailed them to her while I was away. I even planned for one to arrive after I was home.

I would surprise her with a dinner date when she needed a night out. Now having an affair with my wife was fun, but it didn't have that forbidden quality to it, so I figured out how to add that dimension to our affair. Phoenix and Scottsdale are filled with excellent restaurants. Well, we would drive up to one of these places and I would let Jeannie go in first and be seated. I'd wait a minute or two, then enter the lounge, searching for my lover. We would hold hands, looking at each other with deep affection, like people do when they are not married.

Go ahead and have an affair with your spouse and add spice to your love life and marriage!

CHECKPOINT

1. Why are men often reluctant to seek help in counseling?

2. What is the difference between "giving to" and "giving in to"?

3. List the eight guidelines to conflict resolution. How many of these guidelines do you employ?

4. What are the hardest things for you to forgive? Are there some things that you find yourself unable to forgive?

5. What are some ways that a marriage can be strengthened? Which of these ways could be used in your marriage?

—15—

SEX
AND
FRUSTRATED
LOVERS

In this sexually aware climate, with its sexually liberated life-styles, I have some reservations about the need to write this chapter. Everyone has an abundance of factual knowledge concerning the techniques of sex. Everything you have wanted to know about sex is available in volumes of books, explicit magazines, sex-therapy clinics, television, movies, even to graffiti on bathroom walls. Surely one would assume that in this modern age people have gotten it all together at last and are enjoying sexual relationships free of old puritanical hang-ups. The joy of sex is here at last!

From the decades of the middle sixties, seventies, and into the eighties, we have experienced an incredible sexual revolution including casual sex with multiple partners and the flourishing of both bisexual and homosexual relationships. In fact, being monogamous in sexual relations with just your spouse is often the butt of jokes on television. You could feel really out of step if you are "straight" sexually and you are not at least willing to experience bisexual relationships.

The words of John ring in my heart: "Stop loving this evil world and all that it offers you, for when you love these things you show that you do not really love God; for all these worldly things, these evil desires—the craze for sex, the ambition to buy everything that appeals to you, and the pride that comes from wealth and importance—these are not from God. They are from this evil world itself" (1 John 2:15, 16).

A Bitter Harvest

The "craze for sex" has reaped a bitter harvest of sexually transmitted diseases. The "joy of sex" has become the "fear of sex." The fear of AIDS is widespread, especially among sexually active gay men. It has no cure and is fatal. Experts have only estimates that one to two million people have been infected with AIDS. The medical advice for male homosexuals at present for avoiding AIDS is to stop having homosexual relationships.

According to the federal centers for disease control, the nation is in the grip of sexually transmitted diseases that infect an average of 33,000 people a day. That figures to 12,000,000 cases a year, up from 4,000,000 in 1980. At this rate 1 in 4 Americans between the ages of 15 and 55 eventually will acquire a sexually transmitted disease. Millions will suffer from a painful infection that even doctors, until recent years, had never heard of, called chlamydia, with its risks of infertility and problem pregnancies. Herpes, which has no known cure, can plague people for life.[1]

After the years of the joys of sexual liberation, there is developing a sexual phobia where you hear of people who are fearful of sexual intercourse. Casual sex has proven very costly. Yet many people are ignorant or refuse to believe they can be victims of sexually transmitted diseases. For example, a married couple in their thirties showed up at a doctor's clinic in Denver. Both of them had chlamydia. After learning they had experienced sex with other people, the physician asked that they return in a week and bring their partners. They returned with nearly thirty men and women, all clad in the jackets of a swingers' club. They believed that because they knew each other the risks were lower than if they had just picked someone up. All were given treatment for chlamydia.[2]

When I think of how explicit sex, rape, infidelity, and violence come into our homes via television and the movies our children view, I am concerned about such programming and how it will affect their male/female relations when they reach adulthood.

While I was growing up I was very naive, but aware of my sexual feelings and fantasies. There was no television and the sex in movies consisted of romantic kisses. There was no discussion of sex at home. I was able to have a healthy sex education through raising milk goats and watching the times when the nanny goat would be in heat and we would take her to the billy goat to be bred. Then I would count the months and the days when the birth of the new kid would take place. You see I have brought a lot of "kids" into this world. The pregnant goat wanted me to be there when she gave birth. It was there I became awed by the miracle of birth, the process when a baby is born, and how soon the baby goat could stand on its wobbly legs and seek out the mother's milk. Here was sex, so clean and natural, and such a vital process of life. There was nothing dirty or ugly about this sexual process.

Body and Soul

When I grew into puberty, I was filled with all kinds of feelings and insecurities. Taking public showers after physical education classes was an uneasy time, filled with embarrassment and insecurity. Pubic hair, hair under your arms, peach fuzz on your face, the size or lack of size of your genital organs were important to you and your peers. I wonder how many people developed fixed ideas that made them ashamed of their bodies and terrified of ridicule? Women are more sensitive about nudity and insecure regarding their bodies than men. This feeling of shame and feeling ugly about our body is intensified by the idolatry and obsession we seem to have for the body beautiful, the perfect physique, the perfect figure without any blemish. Women are supposed to have big busts to be sexually attractive to males. A man should look like a Greek god who owns his own clothing store, has his own personal hairstylist and manicurist. Since the majority of us don't qualify for the ideal of the body beautiful, we tend to feel less a person and ashamed of what we are physically.

This discomfort and insecurity about our physical bodies is very evident in our attitudes and programming about sex. Sexual hang-ups have been blamed on our puritan heritage, the Victorian age, or the Judeo-Christian heritage.

However, the Hebrew view of creation was that God created man and woman and it was good. The Hebrews had a holistic view of man. The Hebrew word for soul is *nephesh*, which means all that a person is—physically, mentally, the color of his hair, the personality, all the unique characteristics including his favorite food, and his hunger for God. These were all rolled into one being, one *nephesh*, and that was good.

There was no concept of dualism of a body and the immortal soul. The whole man lived, the whole man died. If the man lived again, it would be up to God; and if he died, he lost his spirit, but the word *spirit* to the Hebrew meant breath. How did you know when a man was dead? Check to see if he was breathing. If he wasn't breathing, his breath was gone. In Hebrew the word for breath is *ruach*, which is translated as "spirit" in English.

The Hebrews believed that the sexual relationship between a man and a wife was important. "For this cause shall a man leave his father and mother and cleave to his wife and they shall be one flesh."

The Hebrews also felt that a good sexual adjustment in marriage was so vital that when a man was newly married "he shall not go into the army or be charged with any business. He shall be free at home one year to be happy with his wife whom he has taken." That is from the twenty-fourth chapter of Deuteronomy, beginning at the fifth verse. A whole year, without worrying about being drafted into the army or having to earn a living, just so he could focus on building a good marriage, and a good sexual relationship.

Sex was a very special form of communication and love between a man and a woman. It was a deep sense of communion that was blessed of God, and in the words of the Jewish theologian Martin Buber, it was an "I and thou" relationship and not an "I and it" relationship.

The Hebrew religion was adamant about keeping their religion and their people pure, because of their special covenant with God. The pagan religions were strongly condemned because they offered sex with temple prostitutes as a form of religion.

The real villains in propagating the attitude that sex and flesh are dirty were Plato and Socrates, who programmed the Greek mind with a dualistic view of man. The flesh and the world of matter were dirty and evil. Inside the dirty, evil flesh was trapped an immortal soul that was pure and clean. The soul existed separate from the body and was trapped inside the body until it could be freed by death to go at last to the realm of Ideas.

Thus, when the apostle Paul went to Greece to establish the Christian church, the holistic view of man in the Judeo-Christian tradition was contaminated by the programming of the Greek philosophers. This is why in the early Christian church there was an ascetic movement. If the flesh is evil and dirty, one must control his passions and retreat from the world. So men lived in caves and whipped their bodies with chains. Sex was evil and dirty.

Saint Jerome, who translated the Latin Vulgate Bible, tried to become a hermit and live the ascetic life in the desert, but he couldn't stop dreaming of dancing girls on his chest.

Now if flesh is evil and dirty, you don't have to kill it with kindness. "Eat, drink, and be merry for tomorrow we may die." I know this is much more appealing to us. This was the hedonistic solution to destroy the evil flesh. This programming has been perpetuated from one generation to another and it's about time we got back to the holistic view of man and the belief that the body is good and natural. "And God saw every thing that he had made, and, behold, it was very good" (Genesis 1:31 KJV).

Sex Education

In most families, sex is still not openly discussed with the children. One day a six-year-old named Johnny came home from school, rushed into the house and blurted, "Mommy, Mommy, where did I come from?" The mother was shocked and tongue-tied. Finally she was able to say to Johnny, "When your father gets home, he will answer your question." "But Mommy, why can't you?" She said, "Never mind, you wait till your father gets home." So when his father came home, he was met with Johnny's eager question, "Daddy, Daddy, where did I come from?" "Well, son, I think that's something you should ask your mother." "No, she said you would tell me." So upstairs in the bedroom, behind closed doors, Dad gave Johnny a course in sex education. An hour later he asked Johnny if he had any questions. "Well, Dad, what you have been talking about has been real interesting, but you still haven't answered my question. Where did I come from? Pete came from Albany. Where did I?"

The most powerful sex education children receive is observing their parents express their attitudes and feelings of how a man feels about being a man and his attitude toward women; how a woman feels about being a woman and her attitude toward men; and how they feel about being parents. If a child sees parents touching, loving, and being tender toward each other, that's a good start.

Sex as a Tool

In today's world there are so many thousands of books written about sex that it would seem we should have no real problems. Yet even when a husband has mastered all the artistic skills of lovemaking the wife sometimes feels that she has been worked on by an expert mechanic. Something is missing. Too often sexual technique is reduced to manipulation, or using a person as an object. Where does spontaneity and passion belong? The bedroom problems between married couples are often not over sex. Sex is simply the weapon of choice. The bed is used as the battlefield or the bargain counter where, in exchange for sexual favors, a man will buy a new toaster, washing machine, vacuum cleaner, or drapes. You wonder how many things have been bargained for in the bedroom. It's there that the underlying resentments, misunderstandings, frustrations, and repressed anger surface.

Understanding Male and Female Sexuality

There is a story about creation when God made Adam and placed him in the Garden of Eden. Soon Adam complained to God that he was lonesome. So God created Eve and told Adam that there was a woman by the name of Eve on the other side of the garden, and he should go meet her. Well, soon Adam was back and he said, "I met her."

"Well," God said, "go over and hold her hand and give her a squeeze." So Adam did as he was instructed, but soon he was back. God finally said, "Adam go over to Eve and be fruitful and multiply the earth."

"All right," said Adam. A few minutes later, Adam was back and said, "God, what's a headache?"

I've come to the conclusion that many men are lousy lovers. I know that's not a very popular statement to make, but I do feel that men are ignorant about women. When I say that men are lousy lovers, I'm not talking about their technique or skill in the bedroom, but their failure to understand the psychology of the female, and to learn how to listen and respond to her needs. Men are lousy lovers when they view women just as sex objects to be used. Single or divorced women or widows have one common complaint about men, that if you go out on a date it is expected, as a price for a few drinks or a dinner, that you pay with sexual favors. At a singles' dance a woman told me that if a man buys you a drink, it means "Your place or mine?" This arrogant, selfish, insensitive attitude by men turns off most women. A woman is not responsive to some man who wants to use her to fill his sexual needs. How do you imagine a woman feels on the first date when the man, who may not even remember her last name, wants to talk her into coming into his hotel room to make love; and when the woman resists, he says, "What's the matter, have you got a sexual hang-up? Are you frigid?" Men like these are frankly just pigs.

Men are amazingly ignorant about what turns a woman on and what makes her feel loved, cherished, and valued. For example, because men physically produce semen that needs to be released, they assume that women have the same physically intense sexual needs that men do. If men haven't had intercourse for a long time, they will feel pressure to have it. A man projects onto a woman his sexual neediness, but a woman's sexual desires may rise and fall in relationship to her menstrual cycle, and she does not have the same intense need of physical release.

In recent years some women have been trying to reduce or ignore the basic psychological and physiological differences between the male and female. They say the only difference would be that a woman can conceive and give birth to children. However, as much as I have been talking about the programming of a man or a woman, there are basic differences in hormones, biochemistry, anatomy, and the emotional life. I have never experienced a menstrual cycle, or known what it's like to be one day before my period. I've never been pregnant, and no matter how hard I try to empathize with the experience, I cannot completely identify with it. I do know what it's like to live with a woman before she has a period, and when she has experienced physical and emotional changes of life.

Dr. James Dobson, in his book *What Wives Wish Their Husbands Knew about Women*, writes: "Males and females differ biochemically, anatomically, and emotionally. In truth they are unique in every cell of their bodies. For men carry a different chromosome pattern than women. There is considerable evidence to indicate that the hypothalamic region, located just above the pituitary gland in the mid-brain, is wired very uniquely for each of the sexes. Thus, the hypothalamus, known as the seat of the emotions, provides women with a different psychological frame of reference than men. These and other features account for, beyond deniable fact, that masculine and feminine expressions of sexuality are far from identical. Failure to understand this uniqueness can produce a continual source of marital frustration and guilt."[3]

When a young man is at the height of his hormonal sexual activity, he thinks about sex with women almost all the time. He's easily stimulated and excited, and it doesn't occur to him that women aren't under the same sexual head of steam that he is experiencing. In a few more years he will settle down with a normal sexual rhythm to his life.

A man tends to use sex as a means of solving marital disagreements and tensions, and he doesn't understand what's wrong with his wife when she doesn't go along with his solution. Such frustrations and irritations can build an emotional wall within a woman. She needs communication, understanding, tenderness, and the resolution of conflicts and frustrations to free her to enjoy sexual relations.

It's unfortunate that women have a tendency to hold on to resentments and frustrations rather than discharge them. This creates a smoldering volcano in their emotional life. Women need to discharge these negative emotions so they can give themselves again freely and lovingly.

Men have been told in countless ways that preparing the emotional climate and attitudes for sexual relations in the evening takes place long before the couple gets ready for bed. Now, I know a man who said to me, "What good does it do you to try? Every time I try to give my honey a squeeze during the day, or say something nice to her, or get a little amorous before bedtime, all I get is a lecture. 'Is that the only time you think of me, when you want to have sex with me at night?' I just can't please that woman. She used to complain that I would work out all day in the shop and then, after dinner, watch a football game on television. When I'd turn out the lights to go to bed she'd say, 'Okay, Buster, you've ignored me all night. Now you want me to turn on when the bedroom light is turned off.' Well, she was right about that, but I don't win either way. What am I going to do?"

Expressing Needs

I think the husband and wife need to work on a goal of intimacy in their relationships, so they can learn how to express their own varied needs to each other. During the time of sharing and intimacy, it would be helpful to know that every tender touch or word said during the day was just simply a way of saying "I love you, and I value you; I need you." If a man can express what he feels, listen to and share his wife's feelings, the exchange will provide the right intimacy.

Many marriages suffer from an emotional impoverishment.

The hardworking man may drive himself to be more success-ful, buy a bigger house, buy new things for his wife, and believe that the next new thing will bring her happiness, only to discover that happiness and love isn't with things, but with the person you love.

The greatest gift is the gift of self and understanding. Some of the most tender and romantic moments in a couple's life can be when a husband recognizes how fatigued his wife is at the end of the day. It isn't easy to have to be all things to different people, even if they are your own children, pulling at you in different directions and demanding one more need after another. So at night, a husband might just hold his wife in his arms and say, "Let's just be close tonight. Remember, this is just for intimacy. I don't expect to have intercourse tonight, but I just want you to know I hear you and know you hurt, and I want to be tender with you." This will help a woman appreciate her man as a real lover.

The Little Things

There is a old cliché that little things mean a lot to a woman. If a man tunes into only the content level of the message, he will miss the whole point of the truth He will think, "Well . . . if that's true, I'll give the little woman a blender instead of a mink stole." Let me use this as an illustration of what I mean. Say one morning when I get up, I notice, with my keen analytical mind, that Jeannie is in a black mood. Morning has come at the wrong time of the day for her. I will carefully avoid any involved conversations with her. As I walk out to the garage I notice that there's nothing out of the freezer for dinner, so it will be "Family, help yourself" night, one of those wonderful hamburgers from the nearest chain store.

In the middle of the morning I might call from work to say to her, "I've made reservations for us at your favorite restau-rant for 7:30." Notice how clever I am. I haven't made the fatal error of calling and saying, "Jeannie, would you like to go out to dinner tonight, and where would you like to go?" If she's in a black mood, she will say, "No, no, no, we can't afford to spend the money. We shouldn't take the time. It isn't important. It isn't necessary." If I stopped there and said, "Well okay, I just thought I would try," I would still be in trouble, because many times a woman is saying "No, no, no" on one level, and on another she's really saying "Yes, yes, yes, please rescue me. Please take me out of my black mood and into a pleasant evening."

I have learned—though slowly, I admit—to take the positive approach, and that night, upon arriving home, I find a very vivacious, exciting, attractive, turned-on wife. Now if I think it's just a little thing like steak and salad, and after all I was hungry too, I would never realize the truth of "little things mean a lot." Just one word of caution; if you, as a wife, have had your husband do this for you recently, don't ruin it by saying, "You did it only because you read it in a book."

The Right Gift

There is an art to giving gifts to a wife. There's a secret to giving gifts that will express, on the second level of communication, that you've taken the time to listen to the needs, learn her taste in clothes, what colors go with her complexion and her hair.

A woman will spend hours, even days, looking for what she thinks will be just the right gift for her man, yet one of the most common mistakes a man makes when shopping for his wife is illustrated by the man who goes out on Christmas Eve afternoon to buy a Christmas gift for his wife. He usually will buy her another negligee, or purchase a gift that expresses his ego's need to impress people with his success, or even worse buy what *he* really wants. "Look, honey, I bought you this nice motorboat," when the wife doesn't even know how to swim, and boat rides make her seasick.

I like to give, and I've learned how to shop for Jeannie. I know that avocado and orange are not her colors, but blues, browns, greens, and shades of red, black, and lavender really enhance her beauty. Jeannie is long-waisted, and I know what style of neckline fits her best. I don't always pick the right dress off the rack, but I have more often than not brought home a dress that will fit perfectly. Jeannie is so pleased with my taste in the selection of her clothes that she wants me to go shopping with her when she buys a new dress. She also knows that I don't worry about the price, and I'll buy more for her than she would feel comfortable in buying alone.

The gift of verbal appreciation can chase the blues away. For example, while I know this sounds rather inane, once in a while I will open a dresser drawer and say to Jeannie, "Thanks for all the years you spent in providing me with clean shirts, socks, and underwear." Now she might be a little embarrassed and say, "Oh, that's nothing, that's what I'm supposed to do." And I say, "Honey, I wanted you to know that I'm guilty of taking you for granted too often, and I know that these clean socks and underwear just don't appear by magic."

As a man, find your own words and your own style to say, in different ways to your woman, "Thanks for being you and marrying me."

Emotional Phases

Perhaps the greatest gift a man can give his woman, and the hardest to provide sometimes, is that of understanding and patience. After a few months of living with a wife, a man discovers the menstrual cycle and what a significant part it plays in a marriage. Women can be difficult to live with during certain times of the month. Just before the menstrual period women can become irritable and depressed. This is a good time for a man to have an open door policy with his wife. By that I mean, anything she says or does that appears nasty and irrational, just let it go in one ear and out the other. It also helps if he can shut up and not say, "Oh, it's getting close to your period again."

Menopausal Years

A man needs to be far more educated about the change that takes place in his wife when she begins to enter the menopausal years. The first thing to do would be for the two of you to consult a good obstetrician/gynecologist. Read the material the physician will give you concerning menopause, estrogen, and what to expect, and then ask as many questions as possible to make sure that both of you understand what is happening during this period of time in a woman's life. When a woman enters the menopausal years, her body experiences a period of change and adjustment. There are also psychological factors: fear of losing her youth, her beauty, and her sexuality. These can haunt a woman at this time. A woman can become very nervous, irritable, and depressed for long periods of time. She feels shaky, that her whole world is falling apart. It's not just her nerves, and no matter how hard she tries at times, she can't seem to get hold of herself. This may be a result of a deficiency of the hormone estrogen. This is where a competent physician's help is needed in guiding a person as to whether or not she needs estrogen therapy.

Here's a lit of possible emotional symptoms:

1. Extreme depression lasting for months without relief.
2. Extremely low self-esteem, bringing feelings of utter worthlessness and disinterest in living.
3. Low frustration tolerance, giving rise to outbursts of temper and emotional ventilation.

4. Inappropriate emotional responses, producing tears when things are not sad, and depression during relatively good times.
5. Low tolerance to noise: Even the sound of a radio or the normal responses of children can be extremely irritating. Ringing in the ears is also common.
6. Great needs for proof of love are demanded, and in their absence, suspicion of a rival may be hurled at the husband.
7. Interference with sleep patterns.
8. Inability to concentrate and difficulty in remembering.

This is a time when a man needs to be very patient, understanding, and loving with his wife. But be sure she follows through with good medical help.

What Women Need to Know

Since I've been talking about what a man needs to know about a woman, I know some of you may think: *I thought this was supposed to be a book about men?* So I'll get back to men again.

There are a few things that a woman needs to know about a man. As you may have figured out by now, sexual relationships with a woman are very important to a man. Sexual intercourse for men is a form of communication of love to a woman. A man may not be good at words, so when two people become one, this is his form of expression of intimacy and love.

In recent articles I read frequently of husbands who become impotent or lose interest in sex when the wife discovers what a wonderful experience sex can be for her and takes the initiative in sexual relations. Now this may happen occasionally; but if a man becomes impotent or uninterested in sexual relationships with his wife, I would bet it isn't because his wife's sexual interest and aggressiveness scares him, but that it's another destructive game that this couple plays with each other. This is now his rejection of her or a form of hostility to hurt his wife. Believe me, a man is both pleased and over-joyed when his wife leaves the passive role and is able to participate actively in enjoying the art of making love. The burden of sexual happiness is finally lifted from the man's shoulders and is shared equally with his wife. Sexual relationships can be exciting and enjoyable for both.

I will never forget a book called *The Power of Sexual Surrender*, written by Dr. Marie Robinson, which came out in 1962. I read it, thinking that it might help women and men in understanding sex, but I found her point of view questionable. To quote Dr. Marie Robinson, "In the woman's orgasm, the excitement comes from the act of surrender. There is a tremendous surging of physical ecstasy in the yielding itself, and the feeling of being the passive instrument of another person, of being stretched out supinely beneath him, taken up will-lessly by his passions."[4] This book was written by a woman doctor, and it was a best-seller. Men have the passion, while women have the passivity. Now isn't that a sexy picture?

I promise not to go into a lengthy discussion about what irritates men most about women, but there are a few things I would like to mention. This is the latest scientific discovery about the relationship between a man and a woman: Men are turned off by a nagging wife. Some men have described being constantly nagged by a wife as like being nibbled to death by a duck. I'm sure a woman has more effective feminine techniques at her disposal than nagging. I doubt if a woman ever nagged a man to the altar, but nagging has caused many men to walk out the front door and never come back.

In the same vein, a negative woman is a real pain. Not only is negativism hard to live with day after day, but it's a method of saying to the husband, "You're no good." When a new idea is discussed, an automatic negative response from the wife seems to put an end to the conversation.

In making love, a man needs to hear from his wife what he's doing right, or how he needs to help her respond sexually. Stop playing silent blind man's bluff. A man needs to know if he is a sensitive lover; give him feedback.

Many men will never voice this complaint, but a man needs to feel appreciated and told so. Eric Berne said it a long time ago: "Unless the spinal cord is stroked it shrivels up." Men can become moody, sulky, and cry. This phenomenon has been reported by social scientists. Now he doesn't always know why he's in a bad mood, so interrogating him as to what is wrong will only bring out a hostile, "Get off my back." When a man is sulking, he is really acting out the programming of the inner woman in him, and you, as women, know that this is how women often respond.

Don't make the mistake of using the inner programming of the man; try to help the man get out of his mood. A man can be illogical at times, and if you try to become logical with your husband when he is having a sulk and a mood by saying, "You shouldn't be in this mood, now get yourself together," don't be surprised if he gets all upset. Even if you give him all sorts of wonderful logic about getting hold of himself. Don't needle him or try to tease him out of it. Learn how to be patient, not critical. In other words, give him space and let him have his sulk. You might ask him, "When do you think the sulk will be over?" Quiet tenderness and acceptance will help, and I know waiting is hard for all of us. A woman should remember that it is his black mood, so don't be a blame blotter and overpersonalize it as something that is your fault when it isn't. I have learned to say to Jeannie, "Look, I'm in a bad mood, leave me alone. I will survive, but don't personalize my mood, and don't try to talk me out of it, give me some space. I'll be in my black mood for a while, then I'll be okay." In time, believe it or not, I am normal again.

Sexual Pressure

We have come a long way in facing the topic of sex openly, but unfortunately the openness and frankness concerning sex has also helped to develop a pressure to perform. We're armed with such a formidable array of facts and techniques we are discovering that people are becoming frustrated by the pressure to be good enough as a sexual partner.

"What if I don't have an orgasm with my husband? What will he think? What if I can't have a multiple orgasm?" Meanwhile, the man is worrying, "Does she like my sensuous style and technique? I wonder how many orgasms I can help my wife to achieve? I sure hope I can achieve another erection after making love the first time."

Sex begins to sound like a numbers game. As a result some men feel the pressure to live up to their sexually liberated macho-man mystique, and they become impotent. This is a psychological disaster for a man.

Couples worry that maybe they don't have sexual intercourse as many times a week as they should. Seriously, I once had a man in therapy confess to me that he couldn't keep it up anymore. "What can't you keep up anymore?" I asked.

"Well my wife had a brief affair once, and I felt that if I had been a better sex partner she wouldn't have left me for another man, even briefly. So when she came home, I was determined to be a better sex partner. So we have been having intercourse every morning and evening for about a year, and I just can't keep up with the pace."

I gave him the magic word, "Relax," because it seems people need permission to do that in sexual relationships.

One day a beautiful, married woman came in for therapy because her husband was leaving her for another woman. She readily confessed that she had hang-ups about sex, and that for years she had been warned by her mother not to let herself go and get carried away with sexual feelings. I explained how her programming worked in controlling her personal behavior. I asked if she wanted to enjoy a very natural sex relationship with her husband, and she responded with a resounding "Yes." I gave her permission to let go of her feelings and emotions about sex. She was instructed not to think about what it meant finally to have permission to have sex without restraints or guilt, but she could wonder how good it would feel to express the deep love she felt for her husband, and to realize she had permission to let go.

The next week she came in for her appointment and she was radiant. She said she had never enjoyed intercourse so much with her husband, and he was overwhelmed with his new wife. The affair with the other woman was over and he was home to stay. Two weeks later she came in very depressed and bewildered. "What's happening?" she asked.

"Your depression is a normal reaction, because you disobeyed the old programming of your mother to be careful, not to let go sexually. Now your tapes from your mother are punishing you for being a bad little girl. Your mother's programming to be careful sexually was a way of controlling your sex life. In essence it says, 'If you ever let go sexually, you'll become very promiscuous, maybe even a nymphomaniac, and won't be able to control your passions and desires.' Now you can accept the fact that your mother had hang-ups about sex—and that you are free to make your own decisions, as an adult, as to whether you want to be controlled by your mother's fears and hang-ups or to let go of that old restrictive programming and enjoy a good, natural, passionate, loving relationship with your husband." Later, the husband called me and said, "Whatever you said to my wife, thanks a million."

Isn't it ironic that the old "shoulds" and "nots" which controlled sexual behavior have now been replaced for some people with this new set of "shoulds" and "nots"? The high pressure produced by sexual expectation and demands to be more active and more responsive than is normal or natural have created a new group of uptight, impotent, and frigid people who again need permission to relax and discover the unique sexuality in themselves and in their partners.

The latest reports say that married people do not have sex as frequently as formerly believed. Maybe people are more concerned with the quality, not the quantity, of their sexual relationships.

Relax!

I would like to offer this simple guide to help produce fewer frustrated lovers. Develop the art of intimacy, take the time to rediscover each other as people. Share what's deepest in your heart with one another, because there are no cookbooks on sex that are better than a woman and a man who plan their sexual activity for times when neither is overly fatigued and both can enjoy the goal of sexual arousal and intimacy. There is no need to hurry, just relax and realize that you have permission to be what God created you to be, a sexual person.

Men who have had a problem with impotency need to stop condemning and criticizing themselves for being different. Impotency is far more common today than is widely known. Most impotency is brought on by a combination of factors, such as fatigue, too much stress in daily life, too much alcohol. And then, when a man fails, he begins to play "What if I were to fail again?" and that becomes his own demon. He needs to remember he has learned how to be impotent, and he can learn how not to be impotent.

A good goal for a couple is for both the husband and the wife to agree that for the next couple of weeks they would enjoy the state of sexual arousal without the worry of performing intercourse. Thus, for two weeks the man isn't playing the negative tape of fear, *What if I fail again? What will my wife think?* And the wife will not personalize and think, *What's wrong with me?* The goal then will become sexual arousal, which will reduce the anxiety about impotency, and then in about two weeks or so a man will be able to perform, and neither one will be blaming the other. Be patient and passionate, and relax.

The last guideline is simple and old. If you want to have a healthy love life, don't let the sun go down on your anger.

CHECKPOINT

1. What do you think has caused the heavy emphasis on sex that dominates our society today?

2. What was the difference between the Hebrew and the Greek attitudes toward sex?

3. What is meant by the author when he says, "Many men are lousy lovers"?

4. What are the differences between men and women regarding sexual relationships?

5. What kind of gifts would your wife most appreciate?

6. Openness regarding sex can be both good and bad. List two or three benefits and two or three dangers.

—16—
THEY
CALL
ME
DAD

I've heard many men who are successful in their careers and have reached numerous goals express that if they could do one thing over in their life, it would be to spend more time with and be a better father to their children. The years seem to pick up momentum and intensity as a man forges ahead in his career and his own personal interests; then one day he looks at his children and is shocked to see they are not children anymore, but young adults. They are moving out on their own. Where have all the years gone? Why, it was just a few days ago we brought a baby home from the hospital, and then we turned around twice and the baby is an adult and gone.

The movie and the book *Death Be Not Proud*, by John Gunther, the famous world traveler and writer, tell of his painful struggle to discover his son, who has a brain tumor, before this tumor ends his life prematurely. The agony and the ineptness of the floundering father is a powerful reminder to all of us men who have children who call us "dad."

One of the most jolting statements a fourteen-year-old son made to his father was, "Sometimes I wish you and Mom were divorced."

The father, when he recovered and found his voice, asked, "Why?"

"Well, then you might have more time for me. You're always too busy to spend time with me, except when it's something that you want me to do. Some of my friends have more time with their fathers after a divorce than they ever did before."

That's hitting the man where it hurts, but it does cause him to listen and look at that powerful, needed relationship between a father and child.

Children of Divorce

When a family suffers a divorce, it's a shattering experience not only for the husband and wife, but also for the children. They are torn between a mother and a father, while watching a home disintegrate. It's often after the divorce that a man realizes that not only has he lost his wife and a home, but his children. He's usually living alone in a small apartment with no maid service, and he begins to think about his children. "Have I lost them as well? How can I accept the guilt for breaking up the family, and what do my children think of me?" It is the exception rather than the rule that the children are not used vicariously, or even overtly, to act out the hostility between a husband and wife. Often parents try to justify themselves to their children, saying, "I am the good one and the other one was the person who heaped the devastation upon us."

There can be another extreme that is very confusing for children. In an attempt to preserve the children's love and respect for the other partner in the divorce, one parent may try so hard to be fair that he or she doesn't criticize the other or communicate to the children what went wrong in the marriage. Overprotecting the other can have the reverse effect of focusing all the blame on the protective spouse. Probably one of the most difficult dilemmas is the pressure to choose to love one parent and not the other, while still loving both parents and needing to be loved by both. Often children believe that they are the cement in their parents' marriage, and when the marriage fails, somehow, from the child's point of view, it's his or her fault.

The Sunday Father

With this background, let's take a look at the Sunday father and his relationship with his children. This situation is fraught with danger and opportunity. A teenage girl described her feelings about her Sunday father this way: She anxiously looked forward to seeing her father on Sunday. They would have a whole day to themselves. "He would take me out to lunch, go to the movies, go on picnics, trips to the zoo, and he'd buy me presents or give me gifts of money. It was like a small Christmas or birthday each Sunday. He was so good to me. But then on Sunday evening he would go back to his other life for the rest of the week.

"Mom could never spoil me with the gifts, the time, or the money like my Sunday father, and I was nasty to her at times. Then it dawned on me that it was easier to love me one day a week, and much easier to give me gifts and buy approval because he naturally had more money."

Her mom loved and cared for her the rest of the week, but because of the divorce, money was very tight, and mom was left with the guilt of not being able to compete with the Sunday father. Father may not have been a father before the divorce, but afterward he discovered his love for his daughter, and he felt guilty for not having been a better father before.

The one basic unspoken question that's seldom asked of a

Sunday father, or a father of a divorce, is, "Why did you stop loving Mom?" This is a tough one because a father doesn't want to tell the faults of the mother, so he tries to explain, "Well, we just stopped loving each other."

The next question burns deep in a child and needs to be asked but is seldom expressed. "If you once loved each other, and you now don't love each other, will you also one day stop loving me?"

The Blended Family

There is another category of father. That is the father of the blended family. When a previously married man and woman decide to start a new life together in marriage, and one or both have children from the previous marriage, the children naturally want to know: "What do we call this new person?"

For example, the children of the wife already have a father, or if he died, had a father. Shall they call this new man around the house "dad," or by his first name, or "hey, you"?

The adjustment problem goes much deeper than what do you do with a new man or new woman in the house. A whole new family unit must be developed. There can be problems of authority such as, "You're not my real father or mother. What right do you have to discipline me?" The woman who has been raising her children alone may have developed a very close-knit relationship with them. Thus the mother may be overprotective of her children and the children may resent the intrusion of this strange man into their tight family unit. They may even become jealous that this new man is taking some of their mother's love and time away from them. Thus, the first priority to be addressed by the new marriage is: *How do we accept this newcomer into our family, and since he or she is already here, will things ever be the same again?*

Children need to work out the dilemmas and verbalize them.

"Can I love two fathers [or two mothers], or do I have to love one and give up the other?"

It seems difficult and yet it's necessary to say, "You have permission to love both. You don't have to give up one for the other."

The blended family can become more complicated when there are "his and her children" and then, after a year or so, "their children." If the former mates are still in the picture, it makes for some interesting visitation rights, holidays, and vacations. One thing is certain: Both adults in the blended family need maturity and the decision to love each other with no conditions in order to make the new blended family work. If the man or woman is marrying because he or she hopes a new mate will primarily be a good mother or father for the children, there's a high potential for serious problems that will soon surface.

The Vanishing Father

There is yet another variety of father, different from the Sunday father and the father in the blended family. This is the vanishing father, who just loses contact with his children after a divorce. This is a difficult breed of cat for me to understand. I find it hard to conceive of a father walking out of his children's life. It must be a hard pill to swallow for those children that dad doesn't care about them.

Deciding to Love

Many years ago, in a first-year psychology class, a professor stated that women instinctively love their children, and that a man may learn to love his children, but he never really does love them. I objected to that statement because I knew I would love my children as deeply as any mother could love her children. The teacher was somewhat taken back by my brash statement and said in essence, how would I know I would love my children, since I was hardly eighteen years old and was not a father? My answer was that I had decided to love my children, and I was determined to be a good father.

Someone asked me one day to name the happiest day in my life, and without question it was the day when I was waiting in a hospital and I heard the news on the loudspeaker, "Mr. Olson, *you* are the father of a baby boy." I was halfway down the hall when I heard, "We will let you know when you can see your wife and your new son." I just couldn't believe it, a son. I was a father. It was a dream come true.

When I saw Mike, and then Jeannie, I was never so excited in my life. After being with Jeannie for a few minutes, I began to feel very light-headed and dizzy. Jeannie said they had spilled some ether on her gown and that might be the reason. I'm sure it was the ether and not my excitement and shock, because I soon said, "Jeannie, I don't feel so good; I think I'm going to be sick." I staggered out of the hospital like an intoxicated man, got into my car, and drove to Jeannie's parents' home.

They had not yet heard the good news of the birth of Mike, and that Jeannie was fine and the baby healthy. Thus it was with a great shock and apprehension that they saw me stop the car in front of the house, run to a flower garden under a tree, and begin to violently throw up. They rushed out of the house, and between heaves I blurted out, "Jeannie's fine, it's a boy, he's fine." Well, I was never so sick. I was still heaving that night and couldn't go back to the hospital to see Jeannie and our new son. I'm sure it was the ether I inhaled that made me sick; but did I take a ribbing from my two older brothers about their big football-player brother who couldn't take it when it came to being a father. Really, it was just the ether.

When we brought Mike home from the hospital, we soon got a clue of the awesome responsibility that goes with being a parent.

The first day home he lifted up his head and looked around as if to say, "I wonder what I can get into here?" On a serious note, he became a projectile vomiter. So back to the hospital we went to see if there was a formula that he would be able to keep down, or if there would have to be surgery on the pyloric sphincter valve in his stomach.

Visiting our little baby in the hospital after he'd been home only a few days was a frightening experience for both of us as new parents. Surgery wasn't needed and we gave Mike some phenobarbital a half-hour before feeding him an awful-smelling formula called Nutramigen. Then he was able to keep the food in his stomach. He had to be fed every four hours, and not be held so as to avoid activating the hair trigger of the pyloric sphincter valve in his stomach. It was hard not to hold him, but just to prop up a bottle for him.

The part that was especially tough was at night. He had to be awakened and given phenobarbital, and then there was a thirty-minute wait before he could be fed. Mike, as any baby, didn't appreciate that wait.

I was starting my second year in seminary then, so I decided I would take the night shift, since Jeannie was exhausted with being a new mother. I had made the decision that I wanted to be a partner in parenting our children. I soon became the fastest diaper-changer in town. Mike was a bundle of energy, who didn't need naps. If we were going out for a Sunday drive he would put his head on my shoulder and sleep for about four minutes. Then he would be so revived and stimulated that he'd be full of bounce until one o'clock in the morning. We still have pictures of him in his Johnny-Jump-Up smiling and jumping up and down at 1:00 A.M.

He didn't learn to walk. He started running at nine months. He was an active boy with boundless energy and a short attention span. Also Mike had great coordination, the kind I'd always dreamed about but never possessed. What more could a formerly athletic father want?

He also had no fear. He would dive off a diving board into a swimming pool at two. The fact that he didn't know how to swim was of no concern to him; after all, someone always seemed to be there in time to pull him out of the water. He loved to break away from my hold, and run into the surf in Southern California and come up spitting sand and seaweed.

Danny came along when Mike was about four. We also had problems with his formula. No matter what formula we tried it went right through his digestive system and burned his bottom red. In fact, his bottom began to look like red leather from the allergy to milk. Danny was in a great deal of pain, and the doctor in Southern California could find nothing; so we went to Phoenix for a vacation and saw Dr. Schoffman, who was one of the finest pediatricians. He was also a very allergic man himself and had a special interest in the allergies of children.

We had a sick feeling inside that if we couldn't find an answer soon, Danny would die.

Finally, Danny was able to have a formula of canned meat mixed with water. It was a gross-looking and smelling formula, but it saved his life.

Danny and Mike were as different as day and night. Danny was a quiet boy, one who could amuse himself for hours. He was a thinker. He wasn't a rough-and-tumble boy, and when asked if he wanted to go out and play with the kids, he would often quietly decline saying, "No, I'd just as soon play alone."

When Danny went to the ocean at two years of age, he would sit on the towel, and when he would put his bare foot on the sand, he would pull it back and say, "Ugh," and sit back on the beach towel. He didn't like the feel of the sand. We could have left him there on the beach towel all day and he never would have moved.

Sometimes in the evenings I would go to check on him to see if he was asleep. He would quietly say, "Hi, Dad," and he'd be looking at his fingers.

"What are you doing, Danny?"

"Just thinking."

When Jan was born three years after Danny, we *were* expecting another son and were greatly surprised with a baby girl. By this time we were experts with formula, but Jan had no formula problems; one formula and it worked. There were no problems until she was about a year and a half. She was walking around in the backyard and suddenly fell backward on the ground into a grand mal seizure. We weren't prepared for the absolute helplessness of being a parent with a child in a seizure.

We discovered that with a rectal temperature as low as 101° Jan could go into a fever convulsion. She was given phenobarbital. We aged as parents and hoped that the seizures would become less violent and less frequent through the years. Jan was neither hyperactive like Mike, nor quiet like Danny. Danny would spend hours talking to her in her playpen, and playing with her. She became so close to him that if she ever heard him fall down and cry, she would cry immediately.

Jan grew up loving sports—and what else could be expected with two older brothers—and with a marvelous artistic talent and a rare sensitivity with people.

I believe the most important decision I made as a man was what to give to our children. My family background was a loving Swedish heritage, but there was no hugging and not too much verbalization of love. So I made a decision to program our children differently.

Verbalizing Love

When the children were growing up, I would bathe them and put them to bed, and I would say to Mike, for example, as I hugged him, "I love you for being just you. I'm the luckiest dad in the world to have a son just like you," and I'd also get a big hug back and some loving words. Then I'd go to Danny and Jan and repeat the message. I wanted them to know that they were loved for themselves with no conditions or qualifications. No qualifications like, "I sure do love you, but won't you work harder at school, or won't you pick up your room better?" No, I feel that the greatest gift a parent can give a child is the often repeated message, "I love you for being just you," accented with a big hug.

If a child grows up in an atmosphere that says, "I'm loved for my uniqueness," he learns to trust himself, love himself, and thus to love others.

Now I don't want to lead you astray and give you the impression that I was the perfect father by any means. I had to make corrections in my relationship with Mike, so he wouldn't grow up being an extension of my ego needs by becoming the athlete I always wanted to be. As I said, he had such natural talent and ability it was hard for me to back off and let him be his own person. I became a Little League pitching coach with him, and after two years in Little League, and after I'd bought him new catcher's equipment for Christmas, Mike had had it and quit during the season.

I swallowed my tongue, sat on my ego, and said, "Are you sure that's what you want to do?"

He said, "Yep, I've had it. I'm fed up with it."

I said, "Well, that's okay with me." I must confess that I felt like giving him a long lecture about how important it is to learn to stick to things in life, to build character . . . especially after I'd bought that new equipment. It's hard for us fathers to remember at times that little children aren't miniature adults.

Sometimes it's tempting to give your children all the advantages you never had as a child. I decided I wouldn't force advantages on our children that they didn't want or weren't interested in. If one of them had wanted to play a musical instrument, I would gladly have paid for lessons since I love music so much. They didn't want music lessons, but in time their love of music caused them to save their own money and buy their own stereo system. The point is that forcing too many advantages on children, whether they want them or not, is a subtle message that they aren't acceptable unless they develop these new skills.

I once had a teenager from an affluent family in therapy who said, "Doc, if my parents give me one more advantage this summer, I'm going to run away from home."

A Legacy of Memories

The next important thing I wanted to give our children was a legacy of beautiful memories. Even when I was a compulsive work-addict, I did make time for the kids. I developed a special relationship with each of them alone, as well as in a family unit. With Mike it was hours we spent participating in sports. I'm very much aware that there is a big child in me that loves to play and have fun. With Danny we used to love to play sports too, but we'd also spend a lot of time talking about sports statistics and batting averages, or who was the best pitcher in baseball. Danny is now a walking encyclopedia on baseball. In later years we spent hours talking about medicine and preventive medicine.

When the pressures of college and working twenty-eight hours a week would begin to be a little heavy for Danny, he would bring out two softball gloves and say, "Okay, Dad, it's time to play catch," and this would be his way of talking and getting things off his mind.

When Jan was growing up she was "Daddy's little girl," as well as "Grandpa Roy's little girl." Our special relationship was spending all day on Saturdays shopping, visiting art galleries and jewelry stores, and having lunch at her special restaurant where she always ordered a hamburger with lots of ketchup and a chocolate milkshake. We would walk hand in

hand babbling like a couple of happy magpies and end the day
going grocery shopping.

There is a time in a young girl's life when she needs to be
close to her father, and then when she's worked that through
satisfactorily, she's ready to be close to Mom. This relationship becomes very very special. Later, when Jan came in from
work, or a date, no matter what time of day or night, she
immediately started talking and asking for her "Lady" to talk
to her. It's beautiful to see that kind of relationship.

Vacations were a special time in our family. In the ministry
the best benefit was a month's paid vacation. In the years that
I've been teaching human communication to dentists, we've
been able to take yearly trips to Maui, Hawaii, for two or three
weeks. I would tell the kids that I was borrowing the money
for the trip, but I would rather leave a legacy of beautiful
memories than money. All of us are rich in memories of these
special times . . . the snorkeling, surfing on knee-boards,
building sand castles, and just being together.

Oh, I carry some guilt that I didn't spend enough time, and
there were times that I didn't let them know I was ready to
listen to anything they had to say, but I'm thankful that I
didn't start traveling until the kids were just about grown. I
will never forget the first time I came home after being gone
for a month on a promotional tour for a book. Mike was
twenty-two at the time. As I got into the car I saw a glossy
print of me in the front seat of the car. "What's that doing
there, Mike?"

"Oh, that's just in case I'd forgotten what you looked like."

"Hey," I said, "that hurts."

"Well, Dad, I thought of carrying it into the airport, and
looking at the people to see if I could find somebody who
looked like you."

The next day, Jan, then sixteen, said, "Dad, will you step
into my bedroom and Mom stay out?" Then she started to cry
and tell me she was so depressed that she was going to flunk

a Spanish test the next day. She wasn't going to turn in her homework for math, and she was going to flunk the next test, and she didn't care if she finished this year in school.

I said, "Jan, have you missed me that much?" Then the tears came in torrents and we hugged each other for a long time. I asked her, "What time do the stores open tomorrow?"

She wiped a few tears away, somewhat startled, and said, "Nine-thirty."

"Where would you like to start shopping?" Her face lit up and she wiped away her tears and told me where. About five-thirty that next evening we came home; she was out of her depression. School was not her problem; I was. What was important wasn't the tests or the homework, but that we get together.

Loving Parents

It's often been said that one of the most important things a father can do for his children is to love their mother. This is so true. When they were growing up, I wanted our children to know that, as important as they were in the family, the man they called "father" and the woman they called "mother," were husband and wife, and lovers too. We would fight for times to be alone together. We'd tell our kids, "Don't bug us. Leave us alone so we can talk together uninterrupted." Well, they would test the firmness of our boundaries, and finally when they realized that we needed and wanted this time alone, they would turn away, walk, look back over their shoulders, and say, "Lovers." They got the message. Fathers and mothers are lovers too.

The Need for Patience

I've learned how to be patient, although I'm human enough, and I do blow my cool. When I would make a fool of myself and blow up, I would go to the one I'd offended and say, "Hey, would you forgive me? I'm sorry I overreacted. I have no excuse."

Being so ready to forgive, they'd say, "Sure, Dad, I forgive you. We know you're weird at times, but we love you." Kids are such great big erasers. They wipe the slate clean and forgive. I wonder what happens to our erasers when we grow up, and why we don't forgive and forget and wipe the slate clean.

With patience I've learned to give the young people the space to flounder for a while and still believe in them. This was hard for me, because you don't always know if you've done a good job until the child is grown.

Mike, when he was about fifteen or sixteen, wanted to buy his own car, but he and money didn't seem to stay together very long. He had a job working as a carry-out boy in a grocery store, and I said, "Okay, Mike, you start saving some money and we'll talk about getting your own car."

The weeks and months went by, and he'd say, "Hey, Dad, I'd sure like to have a car."

I'd say, "Mike, how much money have you saved?"

"Well, I haven't got any saved yet, but I'd sure like a car." Another month went by, and I came home from work, and he said, "Hey, Dad, look what I've got."

I said, "What's that?"

"It's a stereo set for my new car."

"But son, you don't have a car yet, what are you going to put the stereo set in?"

"Oh," he said. "Well, gosh, I don't know, I guess I'll put it in Lady's car. I'd sure like a new car, Dad."

I said, "I know you would, son. Let me know how much money you have saved."

Finally three or four months later he came to me and said, "Dad, I'd sure like to have a new car."

"I'd sure like to have you have a new car," I said. "How much money have you saved?"

He said, "About eight hundred dollars."

I said, "Son, then it's time we looked for a new car today."

Mike also tested our patience because his high school group believed that failing was beautiful. We patiently watched while he stumbled and floundered through his freshman year in high school. We hoped and prayed that he would pass. Well, he passed his freshman year, everything but French. Then came the year when he was fifteen, and that can be a very bad year, as you all know. We hoped and we prayed, and lo and behold, Mike made it through his sophomore year. He only flunked, maybe, one course. Then during his junior year, his history teacher began to spark his interest, knowledge, and curiosity, and there was hope that "Hey, Mike might graduate from high school." Sure enough, he did; and then, by golly, he went on to college, and after a year out of college he went to graduate school. It's hard having patience to let a child grow, but it's worth it.

Danny—you know, the quiet one, the shy one, the thinker, the one who wouldn't venture off the beach towel—has spent summers in Nicaragua, Guatemala, and Paraguay as a paramedic for Amigos de las Americas. I guess what I'm saying is this: that when you love, trust, encourage, give lots of listening, lots of patience and truthfulness, your children will grow into unique, beautiful people. Each one is very much his own person and has come to terms with the price of loneliness in those years of going through school. I'm very proud of them.

When Mike was in high school, the drug culture was exploding like gangbusters, and I was very visible in the community giving drug-abuse speeches, appearing on television, and talking in high schools. He looked like me, and I was tempted to say, "Now, son, don't do anything to disgrace your father and jeopardize the work that I'm doing." But I didn't have to because he came to me. "Dad, don't worry about me. I'll never do anything to disgrace you and your work because I believe in what you are doing. I don't want to hurt you. I love you too much." He had four very lonely years in high school.

When Jan entered high school I wanted to have a father and daughter talk with her, only to discover that her two older brothers had each had their own private talks with her about the facts of life. They had really covered the waterfront with her. Each of them told her that she was a great person, but that she would have to come to terms with loneliness as a price for being her own person, rather than doing otherwise and being the most popular girl around and going with the crowd. When I asked Danny how he felt about Jan, he said, "Don't worry about her, Dad. She's her own person. No one can talk her into anything she doesn't believe is right."

This has been a very emotional chapter for me to write. My paper has been wet with my tears. Maybe you're tired of hearing a man ramble on about what neat kids he has. My mind has been flooded with beautiful memories of babies and watching them grow, pictures of a little girl and daddy shopping, two boys and their dad playing softball and surfing, and holiday seasons.

The children are all married now, and a few years ago our first grandchild was born. I must confess that at first I was uncomfortable with seeing myself as a grandfather and sleeping with a grandmother. But that soon passed. I love to be with my grandchildren and they love the stories I make up about those rabbits, "Thumper," "Bumper," and "Stumper." In this season of my life, I love my new title, "Grandpa Ken."

CHECKPOINT

1. What are some of the problems that children of a divorced couple encounter?

2. The author says, "I believe the most important decision I made as a man was what to give to our children." What did he give them?

3. What legacies have you left with your children?

4. What have you felt were the most meaningful times in your family's experiences? What made them so meaningful?

5. "One of the most important things a father can do for his children is to love their mother." Why is this so important to children?

CONCLUSION

part five

—17—

SPIRITUALLY ALIVE

"Then God said, 'Let us make a man—someone like ourselves . . .' " (Genesis 1:26).

God is like a deep-sea diver who is always searching for the lost treasures of sunken ships. He searches until He finds something of value like coins that hardly look like coins because of the encrustation of coral, barnacles, and oxidation over time. God knows there is something of value beneath the encrustation. That something of value is you and I who were created in the likeness and image of God. God is a spirit and we are spiritual at the core of our being. God created us to be very special when we were made in His image.

God is love. We were created out of love and for love and to respond to God in love. His desire was to have communion and communication with us, but like the lost coins of a sunken ship, we don't resemble what we were created for, and we are covered with a lot of junk that hides the image on the coin.

My spiritual pilgrimage has been to get rid of the "junk" or "barnacles" I have picked up in living so I can become spiritually alive as a man and respond to the God in whose image I was created as a child of God.

The apostle Paul writes, "When I was a child, I spoke and thought and reasoned as a child does. But when I became a man my thoughts grew far beyond those of my childhood and now I have put away childish things" (1 Corinthians 13:11).

A Childlike Faith

In some ways these words of Paul bother me, because when I was a child I had a deep faith and trust in God. I believed that if I got into any dangerous situation, God would just let down a rope and pull me out of the danger. My mom confessed to me years later that my faith in God scared her because she was afraid I might purposefully test God's rope.

In 1936 we went to Estes Park, Colorado, for a wonderful vacation. One day a group of us went on a hike to a lake high in the mountains. Coming home from the lake our party was divided into two groups. Somehow I was left behind on the trail. My mom thought I was with the other group, but when the two groups met on the trail, Mom realized I was not there and was lost somewhere back up on the mountain. They frantically went back to look for me. When they found me, I was calmly sitting on a rock waiting for them. Mom couldn't get over the fact that I hadn't panicked and gone off the trail. She asked me, "How did you know you should sit on a rock on the trail and wait?"

At six years of age I thought, *What a dumb question.* I said, "Mom, when I knew I was lost I asked God what I should do, and He said to stay right where I was and sit on a rock and wait for you." I remember thinking, *Doesn't everyone know how to talk to God and wait for His answer?*

But when I became an educated man, from college through seminary and a doctorate in counseling psychology, I lost that simple childlike faith and trust in God. In seminary I read and was taught about God, salvation, theology, eschatology, biblical scholarship, proper liturgical practices and all that a minister needs to know to become a pastor. Just think, I received a master's degree in divinity, but I didn't know how to talk to

God nor did I expect God to talk to me or let down a rope if I got in serious trouble. I knew a lot about God, and my thoughts and rational processes grew far beyond those of my childhood, but I didn't know God or experience Him.

The words of Jesus began to haunt me. "One day some mothers brought their babies to Him to touch and bless. But the disciples told them to go away. Then Jesus called the children over to Him and said to the disciples, 'Let the little children come to Me! Never send them away! For the Kingdom of God belongs to men who have hearts as trusting as these children's. And anyone who doesn't have their kind of faith will never get within the Kingdom's gates'" (Luke 18:15–17).

With all my theology and reasoning powers, I had lost "their kind of faith."

Francis MacNutt writes in his book *The Prayer That Heals*:

> My experience leads me to believe that the kind of person who most often receives healing is someone who is open and receptive to goodness and love and truth. I have seen a kind of bright-eyed look, the look of a child, and when I see it, I usually sense that the person will be healed. Sometimes you see that look of a child in an 80-year-old woman; sometimes you see it in a college student. Somehow that open kind of person seems to receive healing most often. The person who has a harder time receiving healing is a controlled person who has to think everything through before acting, a person who is filled with explanations, and wants you to give them too, a person who has furrows in the brow and a critical spirit. Often such persons are very religious and live exemplary lives, but letting go and receiving love—even from God—is hard for them.[1]

The religious leaders of Jesus' day were good, devout, religious people. They took very seriously the study of the Torah, the body of wisdom and law contained in Hebrew scripture, and other sacred literature and oral tradition. These very religious men scrupulously observed all the rites and rituals of the Hebrew faith. Yet they refused to believe in Jesus as the long awaited Messiah no matter how many miracles of healing, and bringing the dead back to life, Jesus performed. In fact it was the raising of Lazarus from the dead on the outskirts of Jerusalem that caused the chief priests and Pharisees to meet hastily to discuss what happened. "What are we going to do?" they asked each other. "For this man certainly does miracles. If we let him alone the whole nation will follow him—and then the Roman army will come and kill us and take over the Jewish government." And one of them, Caiaphas, who was High Priest that year, said, "You stupid idiots—let this man die for the people—why should the whole nation perish?" (John 11:47–50).

Have you ever wondered why such religious leaders did not know who Jesus was and who sent Him? Jesus answered a group of Pharisees by telling them, ". . . You don't know who I am, so you don't know who my Father is. If you knew me, then you would know him too" (John 8:19).

Religious versus Spiritual

I believe the answer to the question is to be found in the difference between being a religious person and a spiritual person.

Religion is man's attempt to go to God through religious rituals, morals, and beliefs about God, to be reconciled with God. The focus of religious activity is on what a person does and believes about God. Religious activity is under a person's control. Anthony de Mello says, "Religious activity is my favorite escape from God." The Christian churches in the United States are filled with all kinds of religious activity, but too often the people are spiritually starved. They know and believe in God but seldom experience Him spiritually.

For me, being spiritual is God coming to me, and the interaction between God and me is a powerful spiritual experience. For the spiritual person, the source of the activity is God as He seeks us like a good shepherd until He finds us. The hardest steps I have had to take are giving up control of my life and trusting everything to God by allowing God to be God. This has been difficult for me because it is a scary experience to let go and let God. I think I have done this, but then something happens and I discover I didn't quite let God have everything, or I took control of my life again in some important area.

It is so much easier to be religious and do religious things and think religious thoughts about God. I can be very religious on my terms. I found out as a pastor of a church that I could be so busy with religious activities and duties that I had no time for a spiritual fellowship with God through prayer and reading the Bible so God could speak to me through His Word.

Pastors are number conscious. Any time a group of pastors would get together, we talked about numbers. How large is *my* congregation, the size of the budget, the proposed building plans, and how exhausted each of us was in doing the Lord's work. The conversation revealed how religious we were and also how lacking we were of any spiritual experience with God.

Eric Fromm writes:

The vast majority of Americans believe in God, yet it seems clear that this belief in God has very little consequence for action and the conduct of life. If there is anything to be taken seriously in our profession of God, it is to recognize the fact that God has become an idol. Not an idol of wood or stone like the ones our ancestors worshipped, but an idol of words, phrases, doctrines. We violate at every moment the command not to use God's name in vain, which means using his name emptily, and not as the stammering expression of an inexpressible experience. We consider people to be "religious" because they say that they believe in God. Is there any difficulty in saying this? Is there any reality in it, except that words are uttered?[2]

I worked very hard as a pastor in writing sermons, calling on prospective members, developing lay evangelism and lay leadership, teaching adults and youth, counseling, and so forth, but something was missing—the Holy Spirit. I was working up a storm, but my energy and perspiration were not the same as the power and inspiration of the Holy Spirit. Was there any reality of God in what I did and said?

The Holy Spirit

I read Samuel Shoemaker's book, *With the Holy Spirit and With Fire* several times. What he said stirred me deeply and created a need for me to pray for the Holy Spirit to fill me and fill our church. There was very little teaching and no training in the work of the Holy Spirit and how to receive or release the Holy Spirit within a person. I was taught in seminary that the Holy Spirit came to the early disciples and the early Christian church to be the source of power to get the church started. The signs and wonders of the Holy Spirit were manifested so powerfully so that the world would know that the Christian church was God's creation and man's idea. Then after about a hundred years or so, God recalled the Holy Spirit, somewhat like General Motors recalls automobiles. The church didn't need the miraculous signs and wonders of the Holy Spirit, because we had the Bible. The age of miracles was past.

The Christian church developed creeds, dogma, theology, rules, and rituals, and with man's reason and organizational ability, the focus shifted from the work of God to the work of man.

I recalled a story of the time when there was a great cele-
bration of the wealth and pomp of the Roman Catholic church.
The parade passed in front of the pope, and one of the priests
said to the pope, "No longer can the church say, 'silver and
gold have I none.' "

The pope replied sadly, "True, but no longer can the church
say, 'Rise, take up thy bed and walk.' "

One of the early church fathers by the name of Irenaeus
wrote in his work, *Against Heresies*, that heretics were not able
to accomplish the miracles of healings that Christians could
perform because they did not have access to the power of God
and so could not heal. One wonders what he would say about
the Christian church today.[3]

I was praying for the power of the Holy Spirit to come, but
it missed me and our church and hit St. Mark's Episcopal
church nine miles down the road in Van Nuys. On Sunday,
April 3, 1960, Father Dennis Bennett shared with the people
of St. Mark's his experience of being baptized in the Holy
Spirit and praying in tongues. It was such a shock to the
congregation that by the time for the third service, Father
Bennett was forced to announce his resignation as rector of
the church.[4]

I was shocked when I heard about what happened to Dennis
Bennett and this highly successful Episcopal church. The
Holy Spirit was too hot for most members of the church to
handle.

I had been praying for the Holy Spirit to come to me and
our church, yet I wasn't ready to receive the full power of the
anointing of the Holy Spirit. In fact, the praying in tongues
scared me. There was a fear of losing control, yes, even to
God, and I also saw what had happened to St. Mark's Episcopal Church and Dennis Bennett. I have often wondered
how my life and ministry would have changed if I *had* been
open to receive the empowerment of the Holy Spirit. I believe God was not too pleased with me for rejecting the Holy

Spirit. I must confess that I have had a greater need to control God than I could ever admit. I could blame it on my Swedish programming from both of my parents. Swedes can be controlled and uptight—emotionally and spiritually.

I look back now and see that my desire for a redemptive church to meet the needs of a hurting world through a counseling center was a safer way to go. I wouldn't make too many waves, and I would be in control of the situation.

Spiritual Leadership in the Home

I believe that men have a hard time becoming spiritual because we equate being spiritual with being weak and dependent. Men are so full of self-pride and being in control of their life, that it is very threatening to give up control, even to God. If men have a hard time letting go emotionally, admitting they need help, how much more threatening then to ask men to let go spiritually and become as little children before God the Father.

Women are naturally more spiritual and emotionally sensitive, yet it is assumed that the man is to be the priest in his own home. In fact, in most cases, it is the woman who is most likely to be the spiritual leader. The man is seldom the priest in his home who leads the family in prayer and worship of God.

Francis MacNutt began to realize that even Christians who go to church every Sunday have rarely learned to pray with each other at home. He began asking Christians at conferences and retreats, "How many of you can remember your own father ever praying with you in his own words?" He found that only about 3 percent of the Christians could remember their father ever praying with them. Now this is extraordinary! It means that about 97 percent of churchgoing Christians who come from Christian homes and committed enough to attend retreats, have never had the experience of their father praying with them in his own words.[5]

Men not only fail at being priests in their own homes, but often at being fathers to their own children as well. Barbara Varenhorst, in her book *Real Friends*, mentions a study that three hundred seventh and eighth graders did, keeping track of the amount of time they actually spent with their fathers over a two-week period. "The average time a father and son were alone together for an entire week was seven and a half minutes."[6]

Spiritual Highs and Lows

My spiritual pilgrimage has had times of spiritual highs, times of ordinary days with nothing much happening and spiritual lows and times of wandering in the wilderness alone.

While I was pastor at Grace Lutheran church in Richmond, California, I applied to the Graduate Theological Union Seminary in order to earn a doctorate in pastoral psychology while I continued to serve the parish. Although I felt well qualified for the program I was turned down. The admissions committee doubted my interest in the field of mental health. I was crushed and hit a spiritual low. I applied at Arizona State University in Tempe, my old alma mater, and was accepted into the graduate program in psychology.

For a while I was angry at God, but most of all, disillusioned with the church. I took my self-pity and withdrew from being active in a church. I was alone in the wilderness wondering why God did not answer my prayer. During this time I conducted some rather lengthy monologues with God. His silence really bothered me.

Finally, feeling a need for regular worship, our family became active in a Lutheran church which was developing a contemporary worship service. This brought a new freshness and joy to the worship of God. I began to become spiritually alive again.

Starting Over

In 1975 I was forty-five years old and burned out as a psychotherapist and lecturer. In being a psychotherapist, one always worries about "catching it" from the people in therapy. I realized I was "catching it" when I was so tired when I woke up in the morning that I would dive into the swimming pool to decide if I would go to the "Shrink Shop" that day. If I came up, I went to work. I realized I was in trouble when that became the means of deciding to go to the office that day.

I was too tired to read any new books. I was too tired to be a good husband or father, and too tired to pray.

I had advance royalties from the first two books I wrote and I was writing a third book, so with my income from lecturing in dentistry, I figured I could close my office as a clinical psychologist and take a three-year leave from clinical practice and do independent reading in the area of healing of the whole person—emotionally, mentally, physically, nutritionally, and spiritually.

I asked Jeannie how she felt about my closing the office and selling the furniture for a three-year leave. At first she was shocked but then she said, "Go ahead. I'm used to your starting all over again." Now these were the years that Mike was in Lutheran Seminary in Columbia, South Carolina; Danny was in his first year of medical school in Tucson at the University of Arizona, where Jan was also a freshman. Oh, well. I always have been a risk-taking person.

The time to read and study were a real tonic for me because when I am not growing, I'm not happy with myself or my life. In the years since I made that decision to learn more about the healing of the whole person, I have grown so much that I have now reached the level of the wisdom of ignorance. I don't know so many things for sure as I did at forty-five. In fact, at times I don't even know the right questions to ask, much less have the answers.

The last area of study was spiritual healing. I began to devour the books written on the subject by people in the healing ministry like Francis MacNutt and Agnes Sanford. My spiritual life began to hunger for God as never before, and it was a good thing because in 1977 I became very involved in a drastic and dangerous adventure. My planned three year sabbatical from clinical practice became seven and a half years, because for four and a half years I became an amateur private detective to help a best friend who was framed for the murder of newspaper reporter, Don Bolles, of *The Arizona Republic*, whose car was blown up by dynamite on June 2, 1976.

John Harvey Adamson was arrested for the murder shortly after the bombing. In a plea bargain he named Max Dunlap, Jr., as the man who hired him to kill Don Bolles because of a newspaper article Bolles had written about a wealthy friend of Max's, Kemper Morley.

The Story of Max Dunlap

I was in absolute shock and disbelief when Max Dunlap was named as a suspect in the murder. Max was my best friend in high school. He was always a happy, loving person, married with seven children. Max was student president at North Phoenix and he had talked me into running for vice-president. We double-dated during our senior year, spent just about every Sunday together. The women we double-dated with after high school became our wives. Max, a party to a brutal murder? Never. I had worked with murderers and sociopathic drug addicts.

Max was arrested January 15, 1977, for the murder of Don Bolles. His name and picture were constantly in the newspapers and on television. Max heard from his attorney that I believed that he was innocent. He wrote me a very moving letter thanking me for still believing in him. He ended the letter by telling me not to come to visit him in the county jail. I went to visit Max in jail and discovered that he was in solitary confinement. There were no bars, just concrete and a steel door with an opening through which they pushed food. In the cell next to Max was a psychotic prisoner who screamed and swore day and night. Max was not allowed to get out of his cell for exercise or use the telephone to call home. This was when he was presumed innocent until proven guilty.

I knew that first visit that I would have to spend time with Max so he wouldn't lose his mind. When I left him that day, we both cried and hugged each other. Max thanked me for coming but he said, "Swede, I told you not to come and visit me. I'm not the most popular man in town to be a friend to, and you have a good reputation in the valley. Your name will be mud if the newspapers and the police find out you are visiting me."

I told him, "I'm not worried about the police or the newspaper because I am more concerned about a friend of mine who said, 'I was in prison and you visited me, or I was in prison and you didn't visit me.' Now that's the person I have to worry about."

Max was in solitary confinement for a year before he was found guilty and sentenced to die in the gas chamber at the state prison in Florence. I would spend two to eight hours a day with him at least once or twice a week. We relived all the fun we had as teenagers and with Max's great sense of humor, we laughed many an hour away.

I had spent hours going over police reports and depositions in Max's attorney's office. I knew he was framed, but how to prove it and point the finger at the real people behind the murder of Don Bolles was at times an impossible task for an amateur detective like me.

After the verdict of guilty, a small group of friends formed the "Justice for Max Dunlap Committee." The next week-end one of the family members of the committee received a threat to the effect that the friends of Max Dunlap should stop trying to help him or else, and that Max Dunlap was a "dead man."

What Does a Christian Do?

We were called and told about the threat on the Sunday after Thanksgiving, 1977. Jeannie was terrified, especially for our three children's safety. We called our kids and talked to them about what I should do about continuing to try and help Max. Jeannie wanted me to stop trying, but how could I stop when I knew that he was innocent? How could I live with myself if Max died in the gas chamber? Yet how could I live with myself if my wife or children were killed? What does a Christian do in these circumstances? What would you do, if you were in my shoes?

Jesus' words about discipleship took on a new, very personal meaning to me: "If you refuse to take up your cross and follow me, you are not worthy of being mine."

"If you cling to your life, you will lose it, but if you give it up for me, you will save it" (Matthew 10:38, 39).

God's love now became a very uncomfortable love for me.

We contacted a security patrol to have our house on twenty-four hour surveillance. I bought "his" and "hers" revolvers as early Christmas presents for Jeannie and myself. We put threads on the hoods of our cars to check for dynamite. In short, we had a course in defensive paranoia. I had never lived with fear before, but then I felt the icy fingers of fear and I hated it. I hated the fear I was exposing my wife to daily.

The telephone began to ring every morning between 8:00 and 9:00 A.M., just one ring, seven days a week, for over two years. Just a little reminder that someone was thinking of us. Also, our telephone was tapped. Sometimes the burglar alarm would go off at 2:00 or 3:00 A.M. The fear of murder put a real strain on our marriage. I felt and hoped that I was doing what Jesus wanted me to do.

Needless to say, I became very spiritual. I prayed to God and read the Bible as I had never done before. In the midst of this I was still studying about spiritual healing. There was a deep hunger to know and experience God. I would serve Him in whatever way He wanted. If I was to go back into the ministry, I would do so gladly.

After awhile I made a decision about living with the fear of being killed. I said, "God, I hate this fear, so I am giving it to you. You take it." And God took my fear away. I quit carrying a gun. I pulled off the threads on the hoods of our cars, and I released the security patrol from the twenty-four hour surveillance. It was great to live without fear. If I was to be killed, I would be killed, but the fear of being killed would no longer contaminate each day of my life.

After a little over two years on death row, Max was given a second trial. The chief witness for the state, John Harvey Adamson, refused to testify, so the state had no case, and the charges were dropped without prejudice.

Empowered by the Holy Spirit

During those four and a half years of being an amateur detective, I continued to study spiritual healing. I was called by God to go back into the active ministry. After seventeen years of being off the clergy rolls of the Lutheran Church in

America, I was reexamined by the church and accepted a call to serve as an assistant pastor and clinical psychologist. My role was to set up a counseling and seminar center at the church—a Center for Living. This was to be a special ministry of healing the whole person: emotionally, mentally, spiritually, and physically—according to the teachings of Jesus Christ.

I had come to realize how little I knew about the Holy Spirit and the empowering of the Holy Spirit to perform signs and wonders. I knew that when I was baptized as a child, it was the work of the Holy Spirit that enabled me to be adopted by the Heavenly Father to be His child. For me to accept Jesus Christ as my Lord and Savior could only be done by the work of the Holy Spirit. I realized further that I needed the empowerment of the baptism of the Holy Spirit to be used by God for healing and that the baptism is not a once in a lifetime experience. For example, when I buy a new car, I don't expect it to run forever on one tank of gasoline. So, too, if I am to have the power of God to do signs and wonders of the Kingdom of God, I have to keep getting filled up with the power of the Holy Spirit.

I had never before prayed with people with the laying on of hands—praying for the Holy Spirit to flow through me and heal others. But the more I became an open channel for the Holy Spirit, the more power flowed through me. The more I was obedient to God, reading God's word, praying for the Holy Spirit, and sharing God's love with people, the more God was able to use me.

It was exciting and awesome to realize that the Holy Spirit was flowing through me and that people were being healed. The biggest problem I had had with psychotherapy was what to do with the person who has uncovered and realized his woundedness. Understanding and analyzing the hurts is not enough. Now I could see people healed of painful memories and wounded emotions through the Holy Spirit.

A Time of Testing

The next part of my spiritual pilgrimage, however, became a painful and puzzling time. Since 1984 I have been going through a time of testing and being purified by the Lord. It has been a wilderness experience of being stripped, humbled, of learning to be obedient, to trust in God alone, and begin to walk in His ways and wait, and wait, and wait.

I had grown accustomed to accomplishing everything I put my mind to do. Then I discovered that nothing I tried to do on my own worked. These words from Psalm 30 described where I was: "In my prosperity I said, 'This is forever; nothing can stop me now!'. . . Then, Lord, you turned your face away from me and cut off my river of blessings. Suddenly my courage was gone; I was terrified and panic-stricken. I cried to you, O Lord; oh how I pled" (vv.6–8).

In 1982 I had begun to conduct evening worship services at the church I was serving. As part of the service, I invited people to come to the altar for prayers for healing of physical, emotional, or spiritual problems. In 1984 I was asked to resign because I emphasized praying for the healing of the physically sick too much. I left quietly because I did not want to cause any problems for the church.

That same year I tried to write a book on healing the whole person; it was a bad experience. My income from lecturing in dentistry dropped off drastically and my clinical practice as a psychologist slowed down as never before. We had to take out a second mortgage on our home to pay the bills. I began to identify with the Israelites wandering through the wilderness.

In 1 Peter 1:7 I read these words: "These trials are only to test your faith, to see whether or not it is strong and pure. It is being tested as fire tests gold and purifies it—and your faith is far more precious to God than mere gold; so if your faith remains strong after being tried in the test tube of fiery trials, it will bring you much praise and glory and honor on the day of his return."

Walking with the Lord

Sometimes I haven't known if it is Satan who was beating me up or God, or both. I have gone too far in my walk with God to ever stop or turn back. My walk of faith has not always been a joyful, positive, prosperous walk, for there have been times of agony, despair, and pain, but it is a walk with the Lord.

Yet, in the midst of this walk in the wilderness, this time of testing and purification, God has used me in healing the wounded and brokenhearted. I have witnessed many miracles of inner healing. I experience the presence of the Holy Spirit as I sing praises to God. I thank God more than ever, for now I see more clearly how the Lord has blessed me so abundantly all my life. I wonder, with a spirit of excitement, what God has planned for me in the future. In the meantime, I will serve Him every day of my life. I am a child of God again who simply knows: "Abba, Father, I belong to You."

Real Men Keep Growing

I am sure that your pilgrimage will not be exactly like mine. In fact, it shouldn't be.

But I hope that as I have revealed to you my struggles, my joys, my highs and my lows, it will encourage you to become a pilgrim too.

My goal has been always to grow as a man, and I can see growth year by year. I realize that I still have a long way to go to become exactly the man that God wants me to be, but I am just excited to be moving in that direction with Him alongside me.

CHECKPOINT

1. "My spiritual pilgrimage has been to get rid of the 'junk' or 'barnacles' I have picked up in living." What are some of the barnacles that you need to get rid of?

2. How do you reconcile the admonition of Christ "to become as little children" with the admonition of Paul "to put away childish things"?

3. Do you think it is true that men tend to be more religious, while women tend to be more spiritual? Why or why not?

4. Would you be considered a priest in your own home? Why or why not?

5. What are the next steps you can take in your pilgrimage?

WORDS FOR
REAL MEN
TO GROW BY

1. Real men aren't afraid to admit they are not perfect.

2. Real men know how to bounce.

3. Real men know that there are no trains to yesterday.

4. Real men don't suffer from hardening of the attitudes.

5. Real men know how to use an eraser.

6. Real men don't ask other people to punch their ticket.

7. Real men forgive and don't keep score.

8. Real men stop to pick daisies.

9. Real men are good huggers.

10. Real men listen.

11. Real men love their kids enough to spend time with them.

12. Real men admit their need of God.

13. Real men know that true love is never cheap.

SOURCE NOTES

Chapter 1

1. C. G. Jung, *Modern Man in Search of a Soul* (New York: Harcourt, Brace, 1933).
2. Carl R. Rogers, *Becoming Partners: Marriage and Its Alternatives* (New York: Dell, 1972).
3. Sheldon B. Kopp, *If You Meet the Buddha on the Road, Kill Him!* (New York: Bantam, 1976).
4. Ken Olson, *I Hurt Too Much for a Band-Aid* (Phoenix, Arizona: O'Sullivan Woodside, 1980).

Chapter 2

1. Thomas Verney with John Kelly, *The Secret Life of the Unborn Child* (New York: Summit Books, 1981).

Chapter 4

1. John Powell, *Why Am I Afraid to Tell You Who I Am?* (Allen, Texas: Argus, 1969).
2. Robert A. Johnson, *He* (King of Prussia, Pa.: Religious Publishing, 1974).
3. Johnson, *He*.
4. Susan Brownmiller, *Against Our Wills* (New York: Bantam, 1976).

Chapter 5

1. Robert J. Samp, "Enjoy Your Work and Take It Easy? You May Live Longer" *Miami Herald*, February 17, 1974.
2. Milton Mayeroff, *On Caring* (New York: Perennial Library, 1972).
3. Jack Nichols, *Men's Liberation* (New York: Penguin Books, 1975).

Chapter 6

1. Richard Halverson, "Perspective," Concern, vol. XXVII, no. 24, November 26, 1975.
2. Hugh Prather, *Notes to Myself* (Moab, Utah. Real People Press, 1970).
3. Ken Olson, *Can You Wait Till Friday?* (Phoenix, Arizona: O'Sullivan Woodside, 1975).

Chapter 7

1. C. G. Jung, *Modern Man in Search of a Soul* (New York: Harcourt, Brace, 1933).

Chapter 8

1. John C. McCamy and James Presley, *Human Life Styling* (New York: Harper & Row, 1975).

Chapter 10

1. Billie Hawks, Jr., "Lonely Voices," *The Genesis Songbook* (Carol Stream, Illinois: Agape, 1973).

2. Clark E. Moustakas, *Loneliness* (Englewood Cliffs, N.J.: Prentice-Hall, 1961).
3. John Powell, *Why Am I Afraid to Tell You Who I Am?* (Allen, Texas: Argus, 1969).
4. Coiin Parkes, *Bereavement: Studies of Grief in Adult Life* (New York: International Universities Press, 1972).
5. James J. Lynch, *The Broken Heart* (New York: Basic Books, 1977).
6. William Buckley, "Love: Committing 'Sexual Suicide,' " *Arizona Republic*, February 24, 1986.
7. John Money, "Playboy Panel: New Sexual Life Styles," *Playboy*, September 1973.
8. Urie Bronfenbrenner, "The Disturbing Changes in the American Family," *Search*, Fall 1976.

Chapter 12

1. T. S. Eliot, "The Cocktail Party," *The Complete Poems and Plays*, (New York: Harcourt, Brace, 1934).
2. Sam Negri, "Secret of Long Marriage Isn't All That Hard to Find," *The Arizona Republic*, September 1 1977.
3. David O'Reilly, "Live-Alone Figures Show More Men Delay Marriage," *The Arizona Republic*, May 11, 1986.
4. Carl Rogers, *Becoming Partners: Marriage and Its Alternatives* (New York: Dell, 1972).
5. Viktor E. Frankl, *Man's Search for Meaning* (New York: Square Press, Washington, 1963).

Chapter 13

1. Robert J. Trotter, "The Three Faces of Love," *Psychology Today*, September 1986.

Chapter 15

1. Lewis J. Lord with Jeannye Thornton, Joseph Carey, and The Domestic Bureaus, "Sex, With Cana," *U.S. News & World Report*, June 2, 1986.
2. Ibid.
3. James Dobson, *What Wives Wish Their Husbands Knew About Women* (Wheaton, Illinois: Tyndale House, 1975).
4. Marie N. Robinson, *The Power of Sexual Surrender* (New York: New American Library, 1962).

Chapter 17

1. Francis MacNutt, *The Prayer That Heals* (Notre Dame, Indiana: Ave Maria Press, 1981).
2. Eric Fromm, *Beyond the Chains of Illusion* (New York: Pocket Books, 1963).
3. Morton T. Kelsey, *Healing and Christianity* (New York: Harper & Row, 1973).
4. Dennis J. Bennett. *Nine O'Clock in the Morning* (Plainfield, New Jersey: Logos International, 1970).
5. MacNutt, *Prayer That Heals*.
6. Barbara Varenhorst, *Real Friends* (New York: Harper and Row, 1985).